THIS BOOK
BELONGS TO:

....

....

Day Is Done

by PETER YARROW

illustrated by MELISSA SWEET

STERLING

New York / London

$\mathcal{T}$ ell me why you're crying, my son,
I know you're frightened, like everyone.

Is it the thunder in the distance you fear?
Will it help if I stay very near?

I am here.

And if you take my hand, my son,
All will be well when the day is done.

And if you take my hand, my son,
All will be well when the day is done.

Day is done, when the day is done.

When the day is done,
when the day is done.

Do you ask why I'm sighing, my son?

You shall inherit what humankind has done.

In a world filled with sorrow and woe,
If you ask me why, why is this so?

I really don't know.

But if you take my hand, my son,
All will be well when the day is done.

And if you take my hand, my son,
All will be well when the day is done.

Day is done, day is done.

When the day is done, when the day is done.

Tell me why you're smiling, my son.

Is there a secret you
can tell everyone?

Do you know more
than those that are wise?

Can you see what we all disguise
through your loving eyes?

And if you take my hand, my son,
All will be well when the day is done.

And if you take my hand, my son,
All will be well when the day is done.

Day is done,
when the day is done.
When the day is done,
when the day is done.

AFTERWORD

CHILDREN'S WISDOM AND GOODNESS OF SPIRIT is a powerful force that can inspire us and renew us when, as adults, our hearts become weary or confused. Children can light the path of healing if only we will let them take our hand and lead us when we have lost our way. "Day Is Done" expresses my belief that the inherent goodness we possess as small children is a precious gift that we must nurture, care for, and sustain as long as possible. If our early acceptance of one another, our pleasure in making and being friends, our intuitive lack of fear and mistrust, and our heartfelt embrace of one another can continue in our adult lives, it can provide the key to unraveling the root causes of the many challenges and conflicts that surround us.

My songs, such as "Day Is Done," were inspired by music created, mostly anonymously, by honest, real folks who, I believe, had somehow retained the wonderment of that childlike spirit within them. Theirs are the traditional songs that have lasted, and that first inspired me as a child. These songs told me their stories of pain and joy, glory and loss—their unvarnished, uncompromised truths. Such songs are waiting to teach you and your children the small and great lessons that helped me, and still help me, find my way. For this I will be forever grateful.

—*Peter Yarrow*

PETER YARROW of the renowned folk group Peter, Paul & Mary is a five-time Grammy-winning singer, writer, political activist, and founder of Operation Respect, an organization dedicated to teaching school children respect and tolerance. In 1982, he received the Allard K. Lowenstein Award for his "remarkable efforts in advancing the causes of human rights, peace, and freedom."

MELISSA SWEET is the illustrator of the Caldecott Honor Book *A River of Words: The Life of William Carlos Williams*. In addition to illustrating many children's books, she wrote and illustrated *Tupelo Rides the Rails* and *Carmine: A Little More Red*, the latter a New York Times Best Illustrated Children's Book. Reviewers have called her work "exuberant," "outstanding," and "a creative delight." She lives with her family on the northeast coast of the United States.

BETHANY YARROW is a singer whose style connects traditional American roots music with the sounds and rhythms of Africa and the Carribean. She performs with cellist Rufus Cappadocia as the duo Bethany & Rufus. Bethany & Rufus also record and perform with Bethany's father, Peter Yarrow. Bethany lives in New York City.

STERLING and the distinctive Sterling logo are registered trademarks of Sterling Publishing Co., Inc.

Library of Congress Cataloging-in-Publication Data Available

1 2 3 4 5 6 7 8 9 10
04/09
Published by Sterling Publishing Co., Inc.
387 Park Avenue South, New York, NY 10016
Text © 2009 by Peter Yarrow
Illustrations © 2009 by Melissa Sweet
Distributed in Canada by Sterling Publishing
c/o Canadian Manda Group, 165 Dufferin Street
Toronto, Ontario, Canada M6K 3H6

Printed in China
All rights reserved.

Sterling ISBN 978-1-4027-7120-0

The text was set in Worcester and Chikita.
The artwork was done in watercolor and mixed media.
Designed by Judythe Sieck and Chrissy Kwasnik.

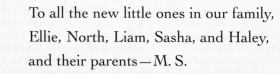

Dedicated to my beloved brother, Andy,
for whom I wrote *Day Is Done* —P. Y.

To all the new little ones in our family,
Ellie, North, Liam, Sasha, and Haley,
and their parents —M. S.

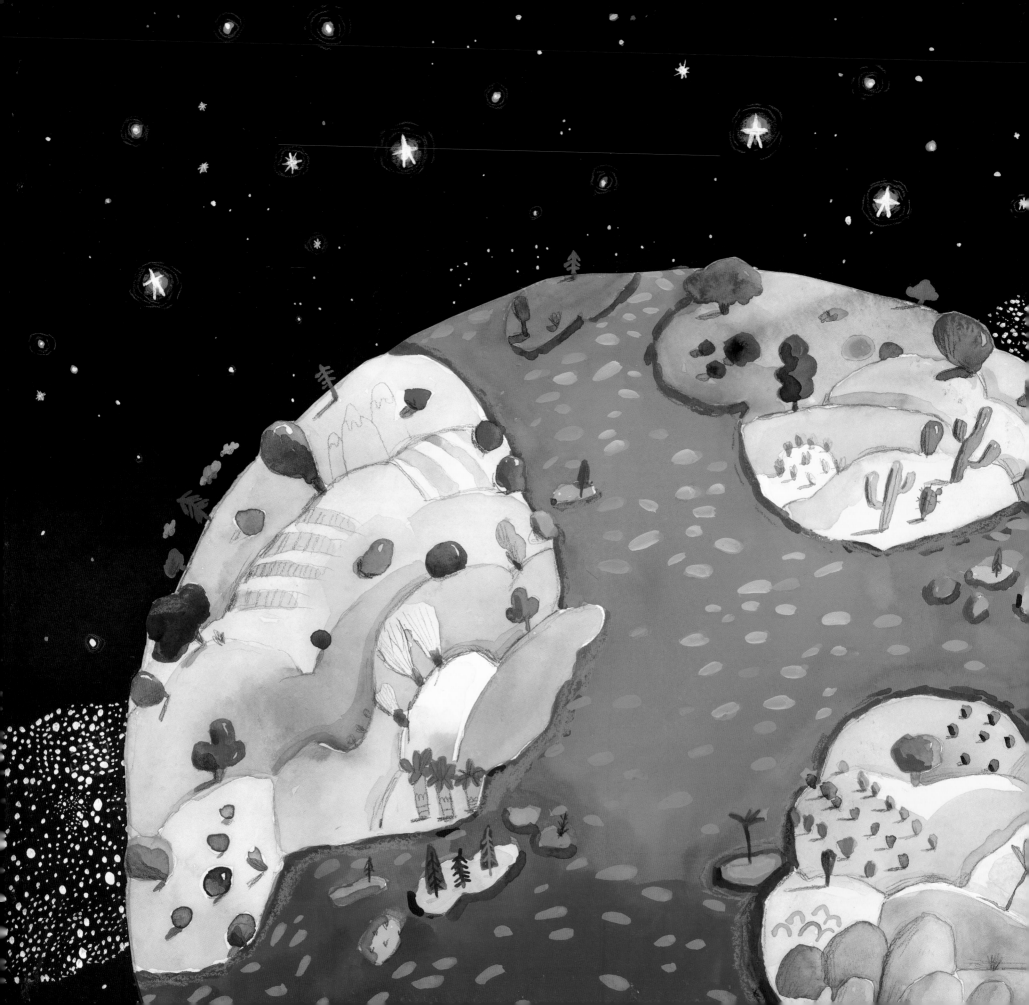

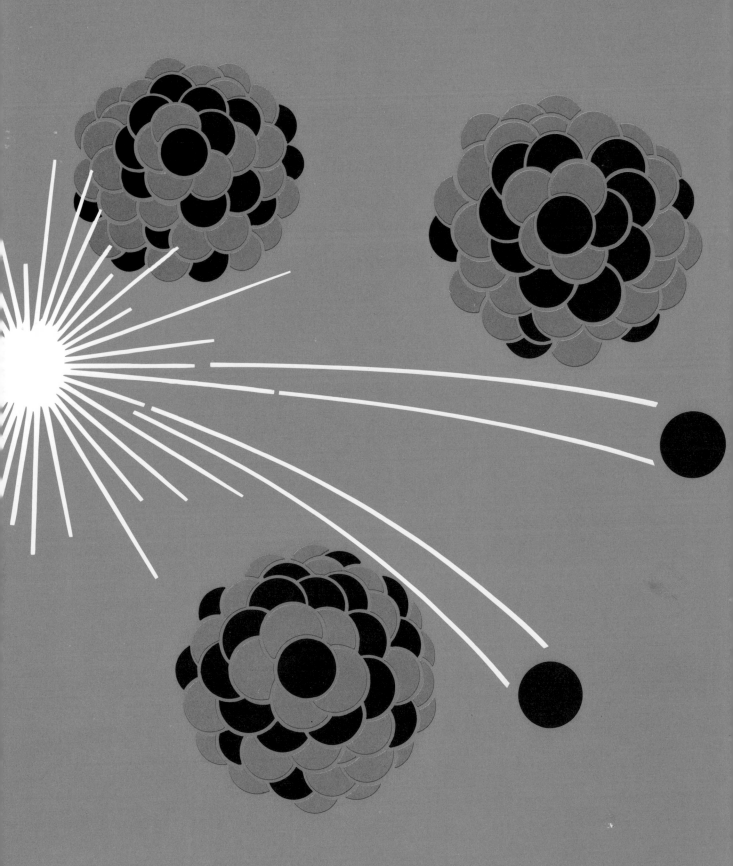

Structure of Matter

TIME-LIFE
ALEXANDRIA, VIRGINIA

CONTENTS

1

The World of Matter

To study chemistry means to peer deeply into the world of matter, where atoms join and break apart, share bonds and dissolve them. A chemist's concerns are the elements, each composed of only one kind of atom. The atoms continually interact with one another, spinning off or capturing the electrons, neutrons, and protons from which they are built.

One of chemistry's great tools is the periodic table, which lists the known elements, broadly grouped as metals, metalloids (or semimetals), and nonmetals; the exception is hydrogen, which belongs to two groups. The periodic table gives the atomic number, which is a count of protons in the core, or nucleus, of one atom of an element. Atoms of an element always possess the same number of protons, but the number of neutrons in the nucleus may vary. Atoms that differ in this way are called isotopes, and they abound in the universe. Atoms may also be stripped of electrons—the almost massless, negatively charged particles that orbit the nucleus—and are then said to be ionized.

Of all the elements, carbon is one of the most important and is essential to life on Earth. Combinations of elements, or compounds, that do not have carbon are called inorganic. Those elements containing carbon are called organic, and to examine them is to explore the very essence of life. This chapter takes a close look at the elements and how they interact.

The stairstep spirals of the double-stranded DNA molecule hold genetic information vital to life. Each molecule consists of atoms *(blue balls),* which in turn are made up of tiny subatomic particles, shown enlarged at right.

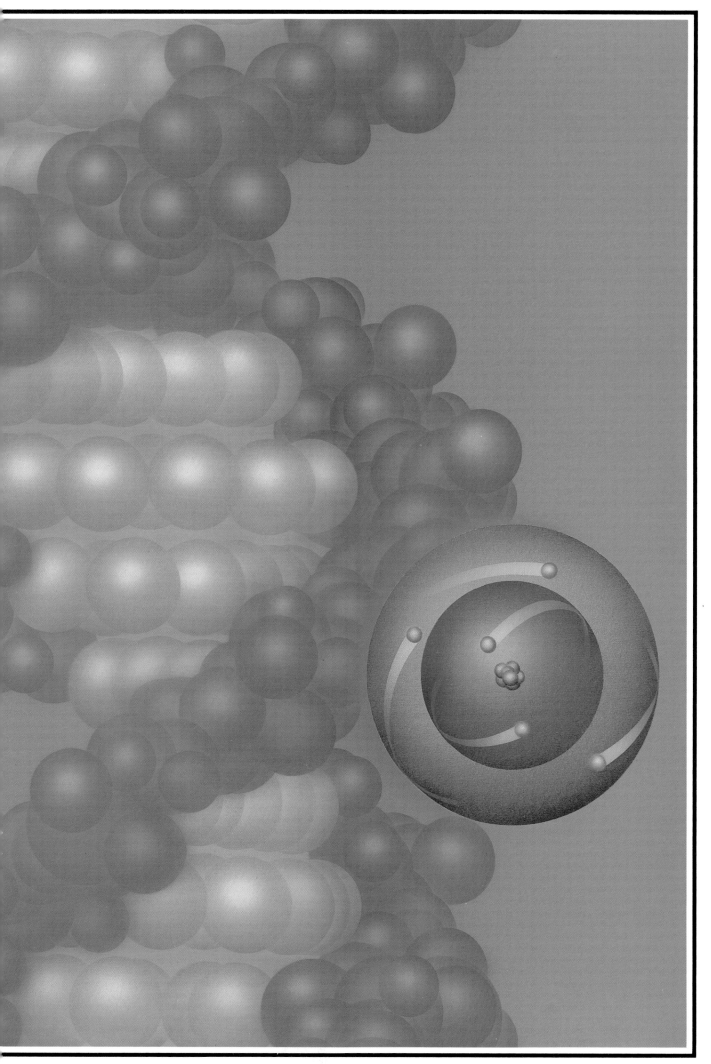

Is Anything Smaller Than an Atom?

Inside an atom

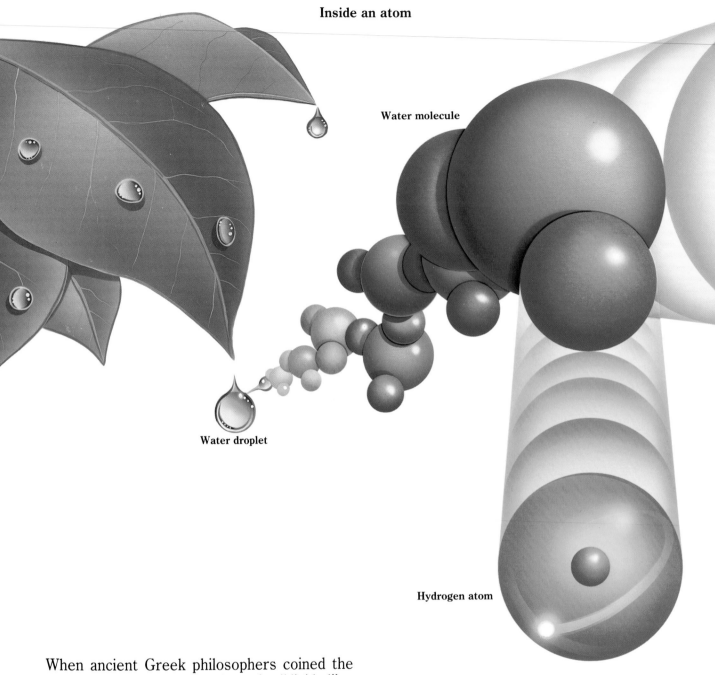

Water molecule

Water droplet

Hydrogen atom

When ancient Greek philosophers coined the term *atom*—*a* for "not" and *tom* for "divided"—they thought the atom was the fundamental and indivisible building block of the universe. But modern physicists have discovered a host of smaller parts in the tiny world of the atom. Within each atom resides a core made up of protons and neutrons, encircled by speeding electrons. These so-called subatomic particles are bound together by two major forces, electromagnetism and the strong nuclear force. Through the power of electromagnetism, positively charged protons and negatively charged electrons attract, while the strong force operates between protons and neutrons in an atom's nu-cleus. Since the 1960s scientists have begun to delve deeper into the atom and have found even tinier units of matter, the whimsically named quarks, inside protons and neutrons. Quarks are about 1,000 times smaller than protons and have an electrical charge that is one-third or two-thirds the strength of a proton's. Thus far, six kinds of quarks—called up, down, strange, charmed, top, and bottom—have been identified, and they are always found in pairs. Quarks are properly the concern of physicists. Chemists limit themselves to examining mainly what happens when atoms interact or join to form molecules.

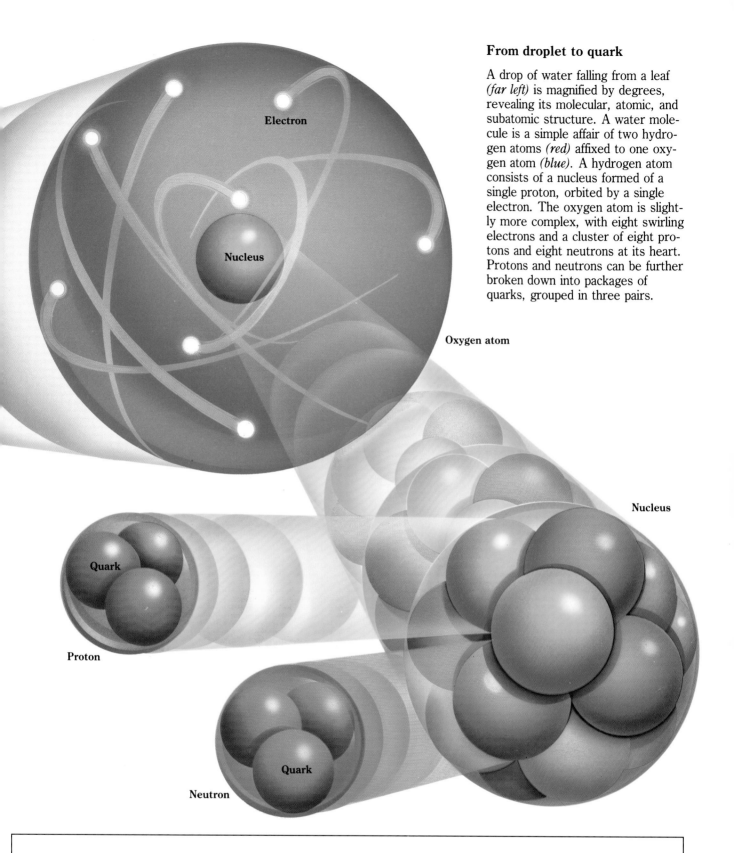

From droplet to quark

A drop of water falling from a leaf *(far left)* is magnified by degrees, revealing its molecular, atomic, and subatomic structure. A water molecule is a simple affair of two hydrogen atoms *(red)* affixed to one oxygen atom *(blue)*. A hydrogen atom consists of a nucleus formed of a single proton, orbited by a single electron. The oxygen atom is slightly more complex, with eight swirling electrons and a cluster of eight protons and eight neutrons at its heart. Protons and neutrons can be further broken down into packages of quarks, grouped in three pairs.

Electron

Nucleus

Oxygen atom

Nucleus

Quark

Proton

Quark

Neutron

Electron shells

Electrons orbit atomic nuclei at up to seven major energy levels. Only a given number of electrons may share orbits at each level. As shown at right, 2 electrons can occupy the first level, while the second houses up to 8, and the third up to 18. These electrons are said to reside in the ground state.

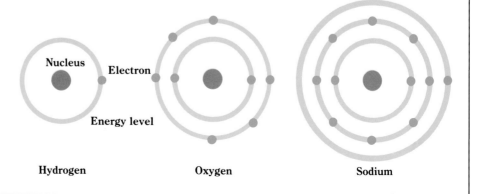

Nucleus   Electron

Energy level

Hydrogen   Oxygen   Sodium

How Big Are Atoms?

Atoms, the basic building blocks of matter, are unimaginably small. More than a million atoms stacked on top of each other would barely be as thick as this sheet of paper. Nestled inside each atom is its nucleus, made up of positively charged protons and electrically neutral neutrons. Negatively charged electrons orbit about this nucleus like planets around the sun. Scientists gauge the size of an atom according to its radius, taken from the center of the nucleus to the orbit of the outermost electron. The range of atomic sizes can be compared to the difference between a marble and a soccer ball. In terms of volume, an atom of hydrogen, the smallest atom, takes up about $\frac{1}{1,000}$ the space of a radioactive francium atom, the largest one. Typically, an atomic radi-

us is measured in nanometers ($\frac{1}{1,000,000,000}$ of a meter or approximately $\frac{3}{1,000,000,000}$ of a foot). Scientists record such remarkably small measures in short form. In scientific notation, 10^{-1}, for instance, stands for the number 0.1. To indicate each further reduction by 10 counts, called powers of 10, the superscript number is raised one count, so that 10^{-2} would stand for 0.01, the superscript showing the number of decimal places. For large numbers, the power of 10 increases the count by 10 times for each number so that 2 x 10^{22} equals 20,000,000,000,000,000,000,000, the number 2 followed by 22 zeros.

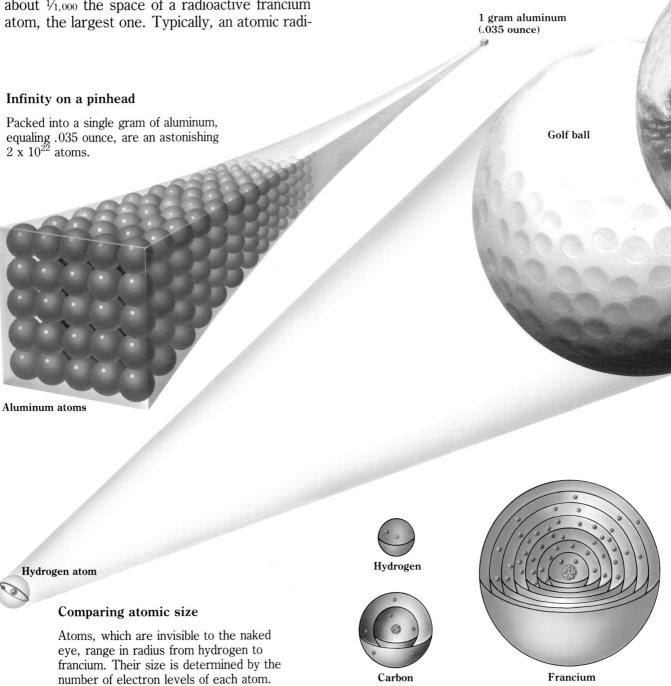

1 gram aluminum (.035 ounce)

Golf ball

Infinity on a pinhead

Packed into a single gram of aluminum, equaling .035 ounce, are an astonishing 2 x 10^{22} atoms.

Aluminum atoms

Hydrogen atom

Hydrogen

Carbon

Francium

Comparing atomic size

Atoms, which are invisible to the naked eye, range in radius from hydrogen to francium. Their size is determined by the number of electron levels of each atom.

A notion of atomic scale

One way of envisioning the size of atoms is to imagine the relationship between a hydrogen atom, a golf ball, and the Earth. A golf ball is as many times larger than an atom as the Earth is larger than a golf ball.

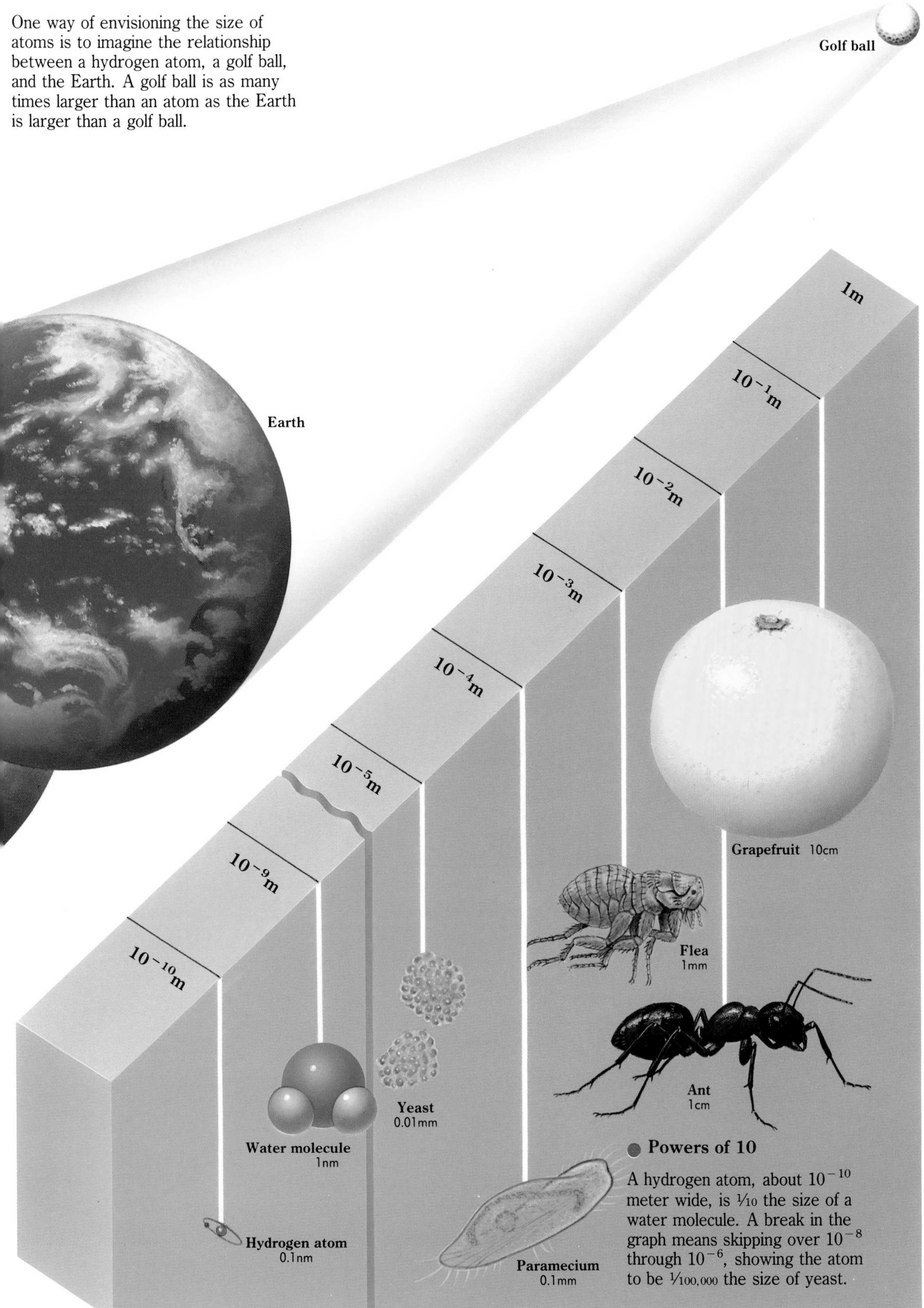

Golf ball

Earth

$1m$

$10^{-1}m$

$10^{-2}m$

$10^{-3}m$

$10^{-4}m$

$10^{-5}m$

$10^{-9}m$

$10^{-10}m$

Grapefruit 10cm

Flea
1mm

Ant
1cm

Yeast
0.01mm

Water molecule
1nm

Hydrogen atom
0.1nm

Paramecium
0.1mm

● **Powers of 10**

A hydrogen atom, about 10^{-10} meter wide, is ⅟₁₀ the size of a water molecule. A break in the graph means skipping over 10^{-8} through 10^{-6}, showing the atom to be ⅟₁₀₀,₀₀₀ the size of yeast.

What Are the Elements?

Elements are the basic ingredients of the universe that cannot be broken down into simpler substances. Every object, from stars to snowflakes, is formed from one or more of the 92 naturally occurring elements; another 17 elements are man-made. Each element has a unique atomic structure that determines its chemical properties. Fully 80 percent of all elements are classified as metals, meaning they conduct heat, can bend or stretch, and are shiny. The nonmetals show greater variations in their properties and include gases, liquids, and solids. The metalloids combine the properties of metals and nonmetals. In 1869 Russian scientist Dmitri Mendeleev devised a way of arranging the elements that reveals their underlying nature at a glance. His method evolved into the periodic table used today, which aligns elements by atomic number and in columns according to chemical similarities.

Atmosphere

Hydrosphere

Lithosphere

H 0.9%

Na 2.6%

Mg 1.9%

K 2.4%

Ca 3.4%   Ti 0.5%

Fe 4.7%

The periodic table of elements

Elements and their symbols

1	H	Hydrogen	14	Si	Silicon	27	Co	Cobalt	40	Zr	Zirconium
2	He	Helium	15	P	Phosphorus	28	Ni	Nickel	41	Nb	Niobium
3	Li	Lithium	16	S	Sulfur	29	Cu	Copper	42	Mo	Molybdenum
4	Be	Beryllium	17	Cl	Chlorine	30	Zn	Zinc	43	Tc	Technetium
5	B	Boron	18	Ar	Argon	31	Ga	Gallium	44	Ru	Ruthenium
6	C	Carbon	19	K	Potassium	32	Ge	Germanium	45	Rh	Rhodium
7	N	Nitrogen	20	Ca	Calcium	33	As	Arsenic	46	Pd	Palladium
8	O	Oxygen	21	Sc	Scandium	34	Se	Selenium	47	Ag	Silver
9	F	Fluorine	22	Ti	Titanium	35	Br	Bromine	48	Cd	Cadmium
10	Ne	Neon	23	V	Vanadium	36	Kr	Krypton	49	In	Indium
11	Na	Sodium	24	Cr	Chromium	37	Rb	Rubidium	50	Sn	Tin
12	Mg	Magnesium	25	Mn	Manganese	38	Sr	Strontium	51	Sb	Antimony
13	Al	Aluminum	26	Fe	Iron	39	Y	Yttrium	52	Te	Tellurium

Ninety-two elements have been found on Earth. In Earth's crust, just eight of these account for 90.5 percent of the total mass. Oxygen is the most abundant element on Earth; silicon is in second place, followed by aluminum, iron, calcium, sodium, potassium, and magnesium. All other elements appear in quantities of 1 percent or less.

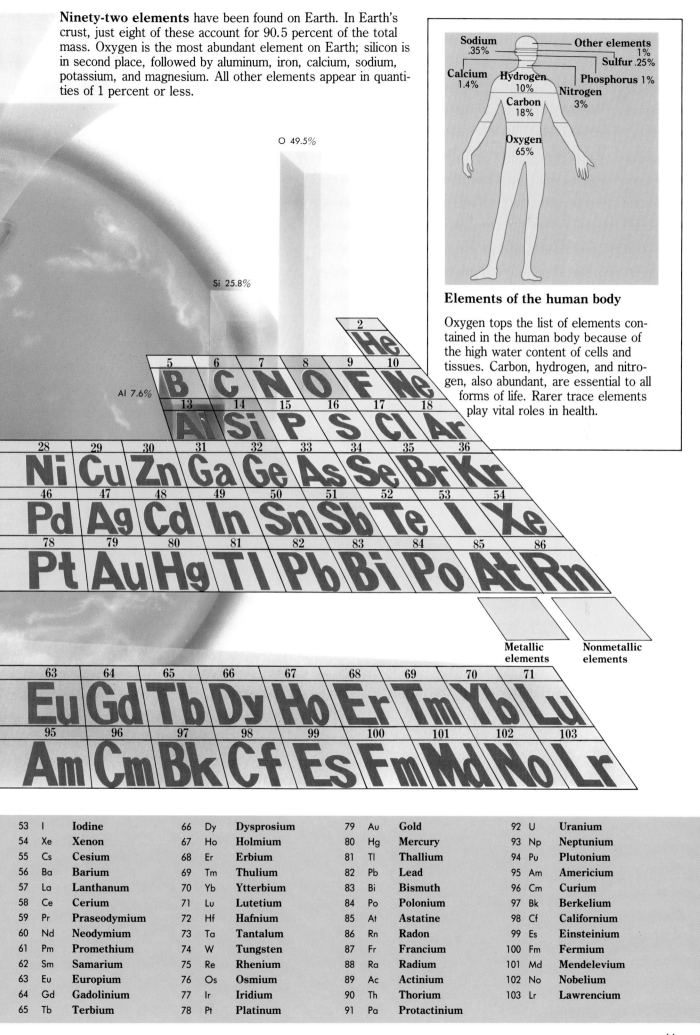

O 49.5%

Si 25.8%

Al 7.6%

Elements of the human body

Oxygen tops the list of elements contained in the human body because of the high water content of cells and tissues. Carbon, hydrogen, and nitrogen, also abundant, are essential to all forms of life. Rarer trace elements play vital roles in health.

Sodium .35%
Other elements 1%
Sulfur .25%
Calcium 1.4%
Hydrogen 10%
Phosphorus 1%
Carbon 18%
Nitrogen 3%
Oxygen 65%

Metallic elements

Nonmetallic elements

53	I	Iodine	66	Dy	Dysprosium	79	Au	Gold	92	U	Uranium
54	Xe	Xenon	67	Ho	Holmium	80	Hg	Mercury	93	Np	Neptunium
55	Cs	Cesium	68	Er	Erbium	81	Tl	Thallium	94	Pu	Plutonium
56	Ba	Barium	69	Tm	Thulium	82	Pb	Lead	95	Am	Americium
57	La	Lanthanum	70	Yb	Ytterbium	83	Bi	Bismuth	96	Cm	Curium
58	Ce	Cerium	71	Lu	Lutetium	84	Po	Polonium	97	Bk	Berkelium
59	Pr	Praseodymium	72	Hf	Hafnium	85	At	Astatine	98	Cf	Californium
60	Nd	Neodymium	73	Ta	Tantalum	86	Rn	Radon	99	Es	Einsteinium
61	Pm	Promethium	74	W	Tungsten	87	Fr	Francium	100	Fm	Fermium
62	Sm	Samarium	75	Re	Rhenium	88	Ra	Radium	101	Md	Mendelevium
63	Eu	Europium	76	Os	Osmium	89	Ac	Actinium	102	No	Nobelium
64	Gd	Gadolinium	77	Ir	Iridium	90	Th	Thorium	103	Lr	Lawrencium
65	Tb	Terbium	78	Pt	Platinum	91	Pa	Protactinium			

What Are Fibers Made Of?

Scientists probe the underlying nature of matter with microscopes, chemical tests, and other means. All substances, no matter how solid, are made up of smaller units, such as atoms or groups of atoms called molecules, which are bound together by chemical ties, called bonds. The illustration below shows how the cotton fabric of a toy panda is separated into its basic components. The fabric is woven of individual threads, which are spun from even finer threads called single fibers. Fibers consist of long chains of giant molecules, or polymers. Each single fiber contains bundles of tinier strands called microfibrils, which are linked molecules of cellulose, a main ingredient of plant cells. The last component, cellulose, is built of carbon, hydrogen, and oxygen atoms.

Anatomy of a fiber

A cotton thread

Cotton cloth is woven from thousands of crisscrossing threads.

Single fiber

Cotton thread

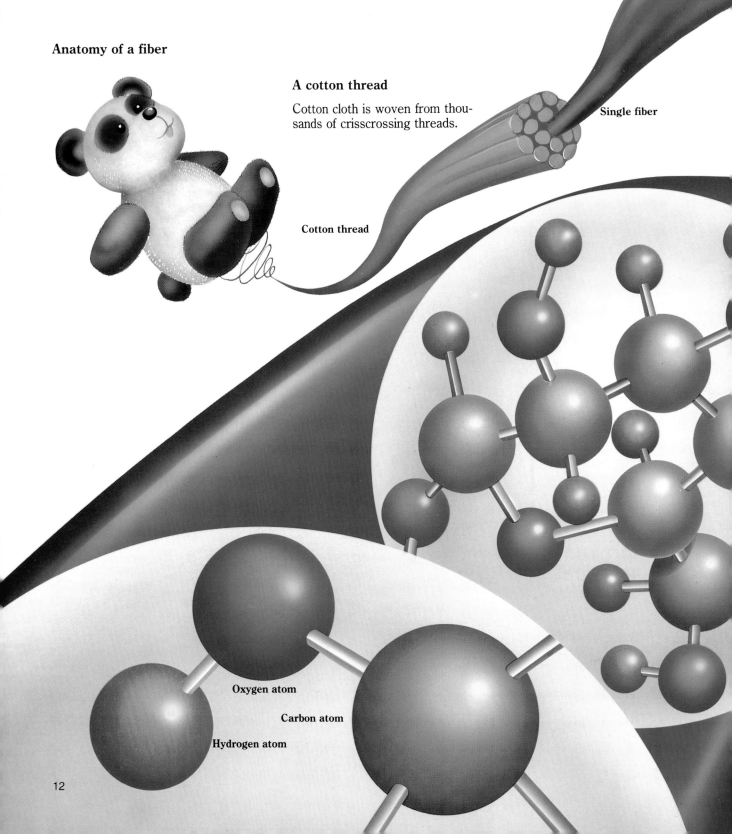

Oxygen atom

Carbon atom

Hydrogen atom

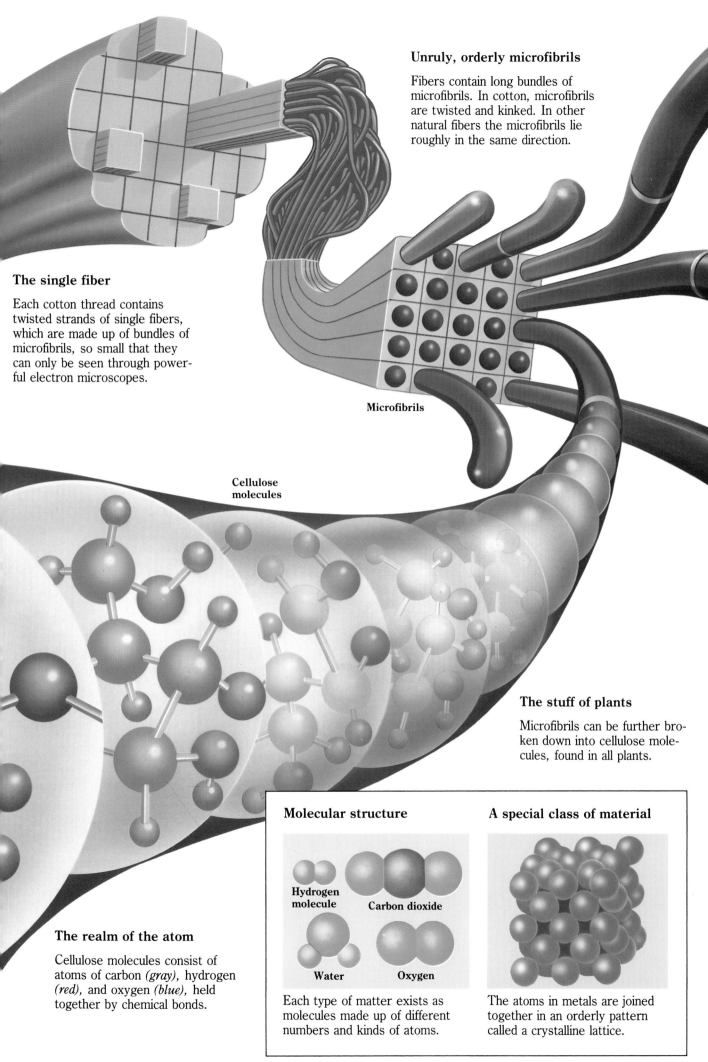

Unruly, orderly microfibrils

Fibers contain long bundles of microfibrils. In cotton, microfibrils are twisted and kinked. In other natural fibers the microfibrils lie roughly in the same direction.

The single fiber

Each cotton thread contains twisted strands of single fibers, which are made up of bundles of microfibrils, so small that they can only be seen through powerful electron microscopes.

Microfibrils

Cellulose molecules

The stuff of plants

Microfibrils can be further broken down into cellulose molecules, found in all plants.

The realm of the atom

Cellulose molecules consist of atoms of carbon *(gray)*, hydrogen *(red)*, and oxygen *(blue)*, held together by chemical bonds.

Molecular structure

Hydrogen molecule
Carbon dioxide
Water
Oxygen

Each type of matter exists as molecules made up of different numbers and kinds of atoms.

A special class of material

The atoms in metals are joined together in an orderly pattern called a crystalline lattice.

13

How Does Nuclear Fission Happen?

Fission, from the Latin word for "split," is the process by which an atomic nucleus breaks in two. Fission occurs naturally in radioactive elements such as uranium and plutonium. These elements have large, unstable nuclei, which decay over time. When the force holding a nucleus together dissolves, the protons and neutrons rearrange themselves to form two new atoms, emitting energy and neutrons in the process.

The emission of neutrons causes other atoms to decay, leading to a chain reaction that prompts neighboring atoms to split. When such reactions reach the so-called critical state, they can lead to cataclysmic explosions such as those of atomic bombs. In nuclear reactors, where fission is carefully monitored, the heat from the fission of fuels such as uranium 235 *(below)* can be used to drive steam generators and produce electricity.

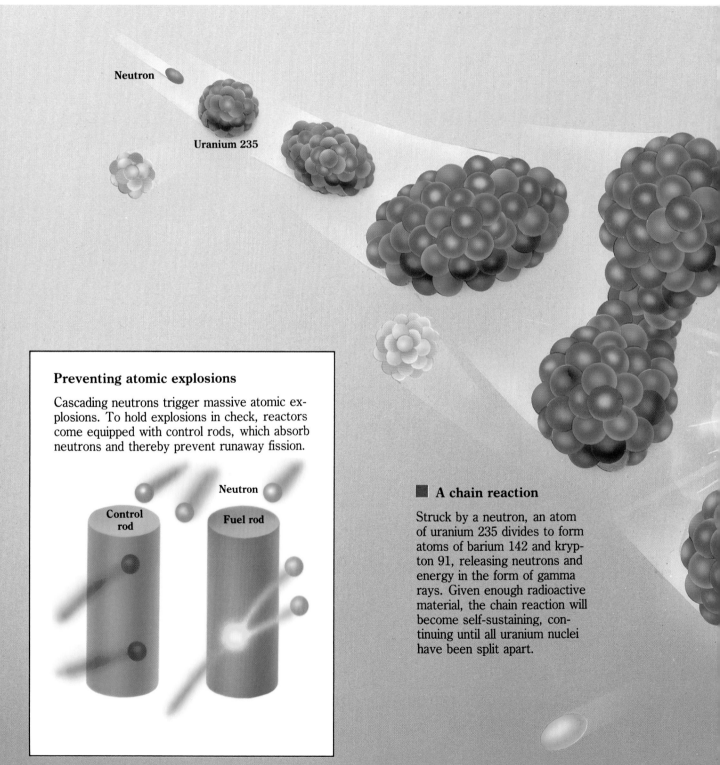

Neutron

Uranium 235

Preventing atomic explosions

Cascading neutrons trigger massive atomic explosions. To hold explosions in check, reactors come equipped with control rods, which absorb neutrons and thereby prevent runaway fission.

Neutron

Control rod

Fuel rod

■ A chain reaction

Struck by a neutron, an atom of uranium 235 divides to form atoms of barium 142 and krypton 91, releasing neutrons and energy in the form of gamma rays. Given enough radioactive material, the chain reaction will become self-sustaining, continuing until all uranium nuclei have been split apart.

A nuclear power plant

The diagram at right shows a nuclear reactor of the type used by utility companies. Nuclear reactions heat water, which flows into a steam generator. There, the 300° C., or 572° F., liquid brings a second supply of water to a boil. The resulting steam spins a turbine that generates electricity. Cooled water cycles back through both systems.

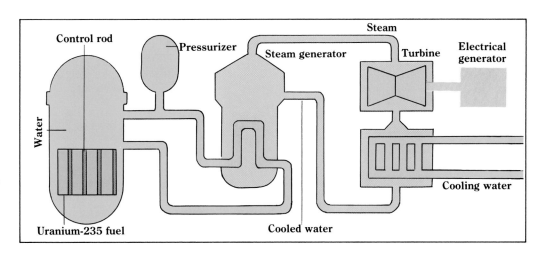

Control rod

Pressurizer

Steam

Steam generator

Turbine

Electrical generator

Water

Uranium-235 fuel

Cooled water

Cooling water

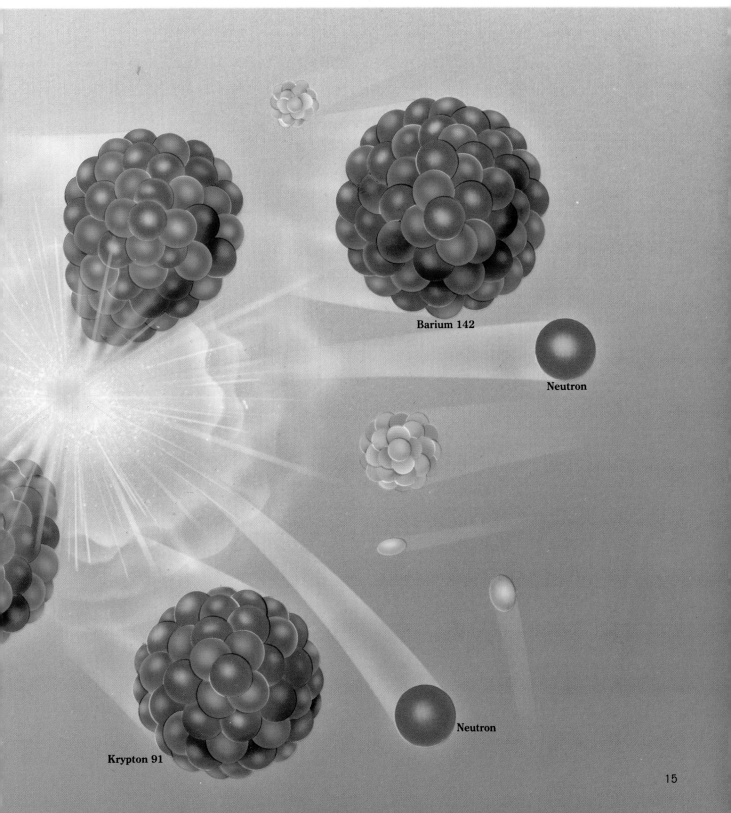

Barium 142

Neutron

Neutron

Krypton 91

15

What Is Nuclear Fusion?

In fusion, two light atomic nuclei join to create one heavy nucleus. This happens naturally within the cores of stars, where pressures and temperatures are high enough to overcome the force that normally causes nuclei to repel each other and to break the tenacious force that binds protons and neutrons. Inside stars, hurtling nuclei fuse when they collide, as illustrated below. A new nucleus forms, and neutrons, protons, and other subatomic particles called neutrinos and positrons are released, as is energy. Scientists hope to generate large quantities of energy from fusion in laboratories and are working to perfect reactors that will reproduce stellar conditions.

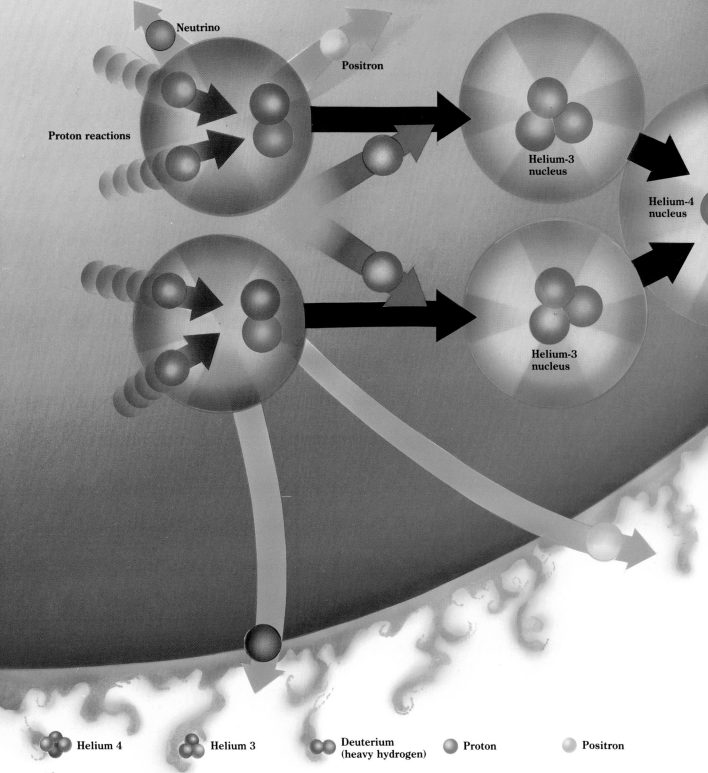

Neutrino

Positron

Proton reactions

Helium-3 nucleus

Helium-3 nucleus

Helium-4 nucleus

Helium 4   Helium 3   Deuterium (heavy hydrogen)   Proton   Positron

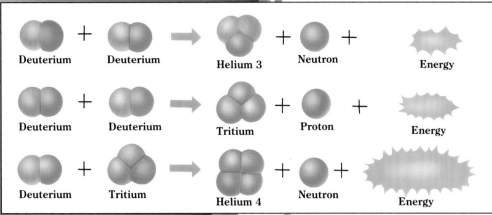

Fusion reactions

Three common reactions show *(top)* the fusion of two deuterium nuclei, consisting of a proton and a neutron each, to form helium 3. The same reaction *(center)* sometimes also produces tritium, with one proton and two neutrons. A deuterium and tritium nucleus *(bottom)* combine to yield helium 4. In each reaction, particles and energy are given off.

Nuclear fusion inside the Sun

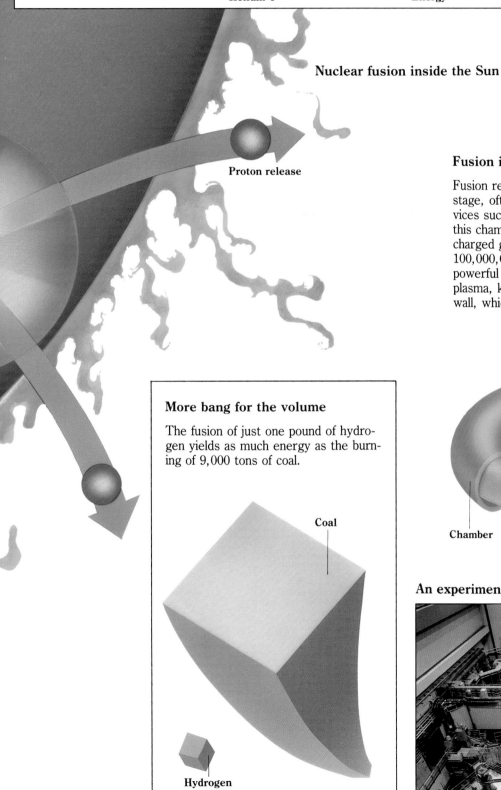

Proton release

Fusion in the laboratory

Fusion reactors, still in the experimental stage, often employ doughnut-shaped devices such as the one shown below. Inside this chamber circulates a plasma, a highly charged gas heated to a minimum of 100,000,000° C., or 180,000,000° F. A powerful magnetic field surrounds the plasma, keeping it away from the chamber wall, which would otherwise melt.

More bang for the volume

The fusion of just one pound of hydrogen yields as much energy as the burning of 9,000 tons of coal.

Coal

Hydrogen

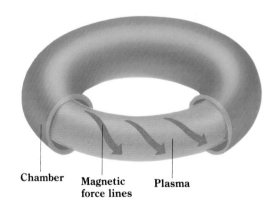

Chamber | Magnetic force lines | Plasma

An experimental nuclear fusion reactor

How Does Salt Conduct Electricity?

Only certain materials conduct electricity. In metals and other substances that can conduct electricity, electric current is produced when electrons slip from their atomic bonds and begin to flow freely. Substances such as salt (sodium chloride) are poor conductors because their electrons cannot move easily. But when salt is dissolved in a liquid such as water, the situation changes. Then sodium and chloride atoms become ionized; that is, they lose or gain an electron, thereby gaining a positive or negative charge, and conduct electricity. Those substances that cannot conduct electricity when they are solids but can when they are in liquid form are called electrolytes. The phenomenon can be demonstrated by placing two electrodes —a positively charged anode and a negatively charged cathode—in a salt solution, as illustrated below. Since opposite charges attract, anions (negative ions) stream toward the anode, while cations (positive ions) head for the cathode, producing an electric current.

Electrolytic conduction

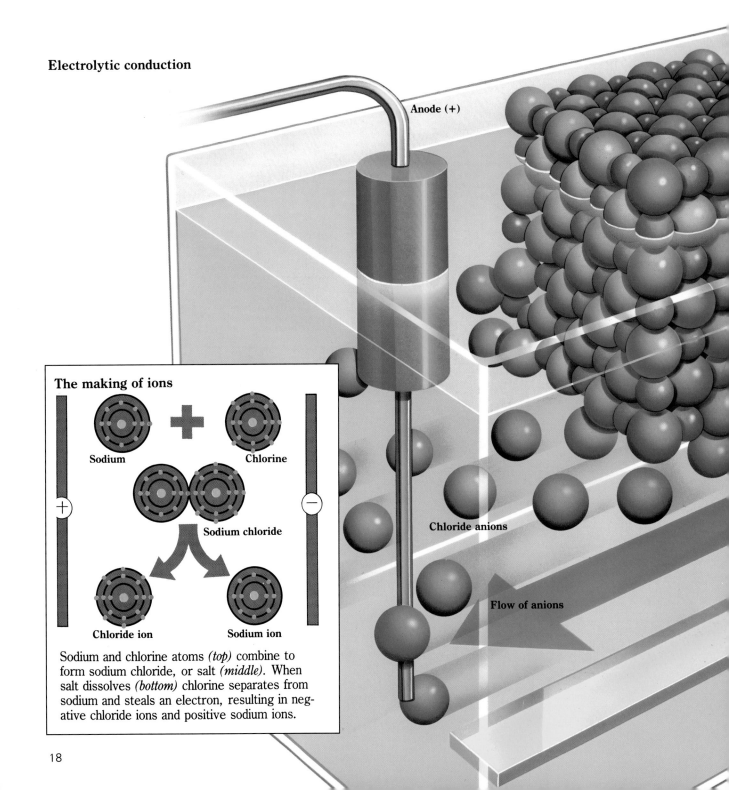

Anode (+)

Chloride anions

Flow of anions

The making of ions

Sodium

Chlorine

Sodium chloride

Chloride ion

Sodium ion

Sodium and chlorine atoms *(top)* combine to form sodium chloride, or salt *(middle)*. When salt dissolves *(bottom)* chlorine separates from sodium and steals an electron, resulting in negative chloride ions and positive sodium ions.

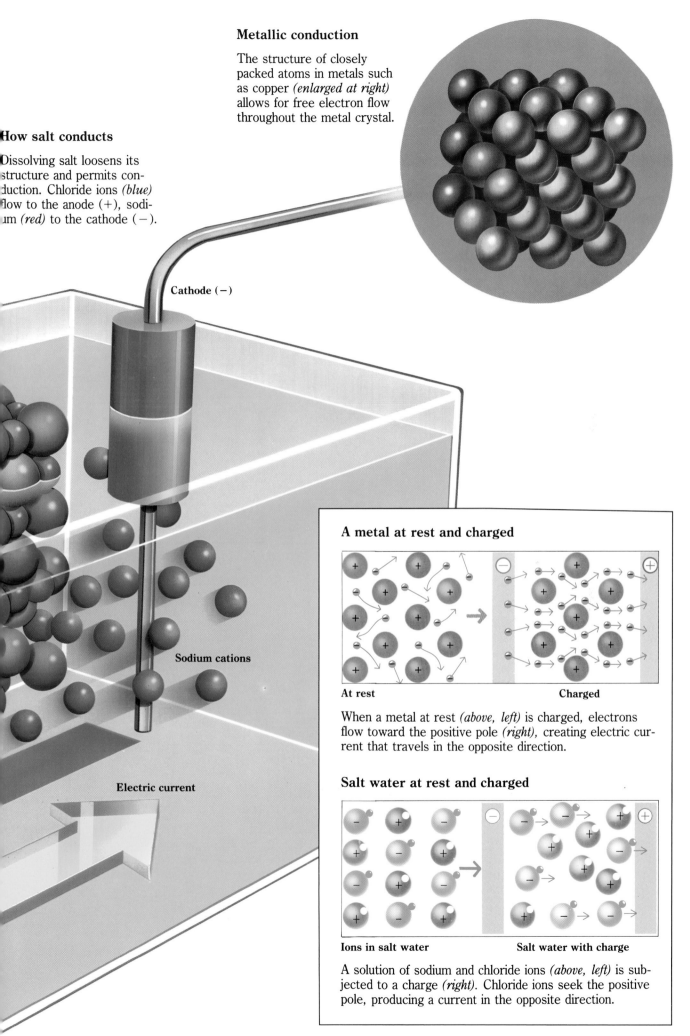

Metallic conduction

The structure of closely packed atoms in metals such as copper *(enlarged at right)* allows for free electron flow throughout the metal crystal.

How salt conducts

Dissolving salt loosens its structure and permits conduction. Chloride ions *(blue)* flow to the anode (+), sodium *(red)* to the cathode (−).

Cathode (−)

Sodium cations

Electric current

A metal at rest and charged

At rest   **Charged**

When a metal at rest *(above, left)* is charged, electrons flow toward the positive pole *(right),* creating electric current that travels in the opposite direction.

Salt water at rest and charged

Ions in salt water   **Salt water with charge**

A solution of sodium and chloride ions *(above, left)* is subjected to a charge *(right)*. Chloride ions seek the positive pole, producing a current in the opposite direction.

How Do Colloids Form?

Colloids are mixtures of substances that have particles of liquids, solids, or gas evenly distributed throughout. The size of the particles is the defining characteristic of a colloid. They must range from .0001 to .0000001 centimeter, or .00004 to .00000004 inch, wide. Depending on their composition, colloids have different names. If the particles are gas and the medium in which they are suspended is liquid or solid, the colloid is called a foam. One example is air that has been beaten into cream to form whipped cream. A dispersal of liquid particles within a liquid is known as an emulsion. An example of an emulsion is homogenized milk. Solids within a liquid or gas are sols, such as aerosols or, if the liquid is water, hydrosols. Colloids include such naturally occurring substances as egg whites, blood, and fog. Everyday man-made colloids include mayonnaise, jelly, foam rubber, and paints. Chemists study the many interesting properties of colloids, including the unique way in which they scatter light or in which they can be filtered.

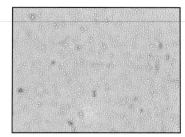

A microphotograph of milk shows suspended particles.

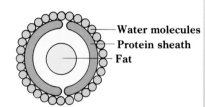

Water molecules
Protein sheath
Fat

A coating of water molecules surrounds the fat molecule of a milk particle. Water and oil do not mix, but in milk, a protein sheath allows for even dispersal of the fat.

Three basic types of colloids

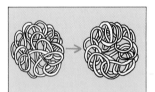

Gas in a solid: Molecules spread out in a network of fibers as they are shot through with gas, creating a foam.

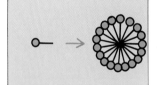

Liquid in liquid: Molecules cluster around particles so that they stay evenly dispersed to form an emulsion.

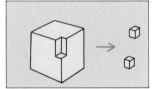

Solids in gas: Solids remain dispersed in a gas if they are broken down into tiny pieces, such as in an aerosol.

The Tyndall effect

Light shining through mist—a colloid—is scattered in bands. The effect occurs because particles absorb and reemit light in all directions.

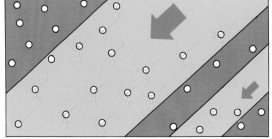

Mist in a forest yields bands of light.

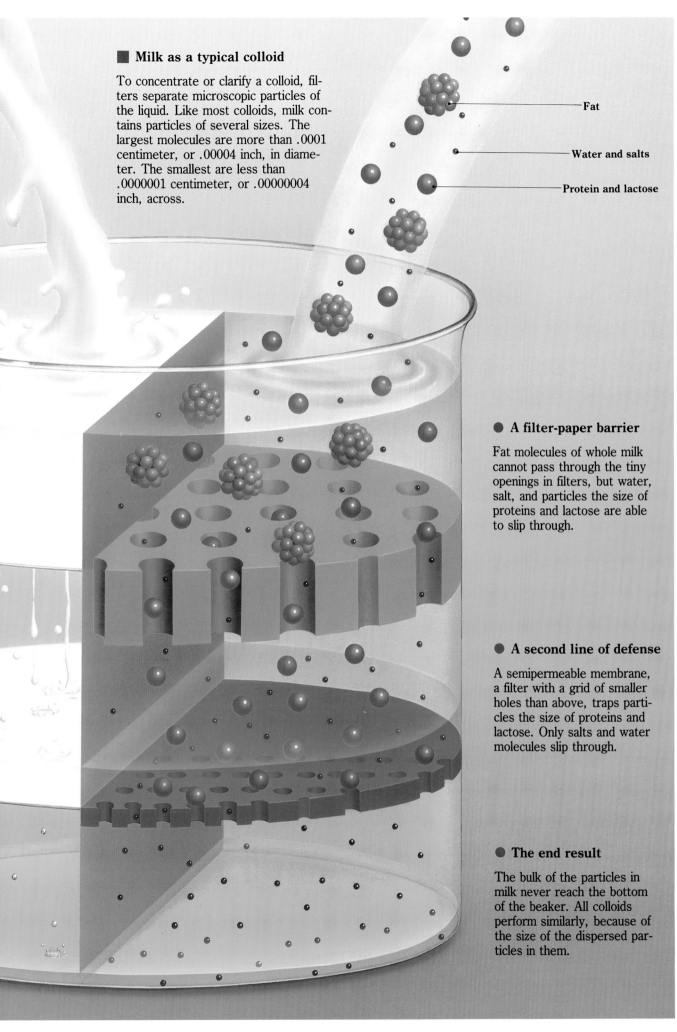

■ Milk as a typical colloid

To concentrate or clarify a colloid, filters separate microscopic particles of the liquid. Like most colloids, milk contains particles of several sizes. The largest molecules are more than .0001 centimeter, or .00004 inch, in diameter. The smallest are less than .0000001 centimeter, or .00000004 inch, across.

Fat

Water and salts

Protein and lactose

● A filter-paper barrier

Fat molecules of whole milk cannot pass through the tiny openings in filters, but water, salt, and particles the size of proteins and lactose are able to slip through.

● A second line of defense

A semipermeable membrane, a filter with a grid of smaller holes than above, traps particles the size of proteins and lactose. Only salts and water molecules slip through.

● The end result

The bulk of the particles in milk never reach the bottom of the beaker. All colloids perform similarly, because of the size of the dispersed particles in them.

21

What Is Antimatter?

Every elementary particle of matter, such as a proton or an electron, has an antimatter counterpart. Each antimatter particle has the reverse charge of its matter counterpart; the matter and antimatter particles are otherwise alike in every other way. While electrons are negative, antielectrons, also called positrons, are positive. Protons are positive, but antiprotons are negative.

British physicist Paul Dirac first postulated the existence of antimatter in 1928. Dirac's theory was not confirmed until 1932, when a scientist from the California Institute of Technology discovered the positron. Further supporting evidence came in 1957 from laboratory researchers at the University of California who succeeded in making antiprotons. Some scientists believe that antimatter was originally created in the Big Bang, the beginning of the universe. This monumental explosion spawned all matter, and mathematical calculations support the notion that it simultaneously gave birth to equal numbers of electrically inverted twins, as illustrated at right. In theory, regions of the universe may be filled with antimatter. Still in search of proof, astronomers are scanning the heavens for signs of a tremendous release of energy, because the interaction of antimatter and matter results in mutual annihilation in which their mass is converted into energy.

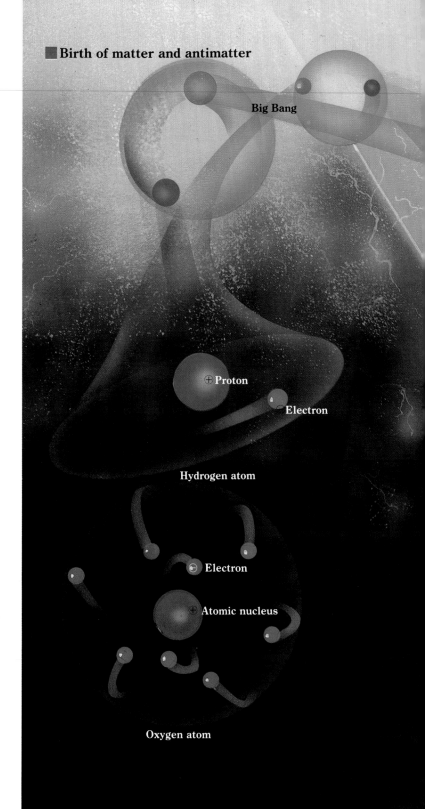

■ Birth of matter and antimatter

Big Bang

⊕ Proton

Electron

Hydrogen atom

⊖ Electron

⊕ Atomic nucleus

Oxygen atom

Positrons

Dirac theorized that gamma rays striking antielectrons turn some of them into electrons *(right)*. The collision leaves a hole, which acts like an electron with a positive charge. Electrical attraction dooms positrons to short lives *(far right)*.

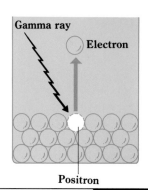

Gamma ray
Electron

Positron

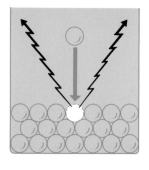

The elusive realm of antiparticles

In the moments directly following the Big Bang, the universe was sown with equal amounts of matter and antimatter. But antimatter particles have mostly vanished. Scientists calculate that the universe today contains only one antimatter particle for every 10 million particles of matter.

Antiproton ⊖

Positron ⊕

Antihydrogen atom

Antioxygen

A mirror image of oxygen, an antioxygen atom *(below)* pairs eight antiprotons with an equal number of antineutrons in its antinucleus, orbited by eight positively charged antielectrons, or positrons. By contrast, oxygen holds positive protons, neutrons, and negative electrons.

Antinucleus ⊖

Positron ⊕

Antioxygen atom

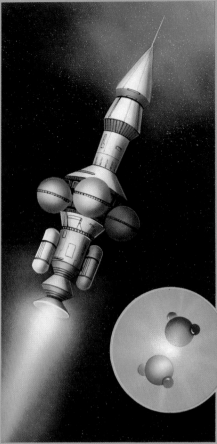

Space buffs envision a rocket that would fly to distant stars on energy resulting from matter-antimatter collisions. This highly theoretical dream is still far from becoming reality.

Antimatter

Matter

A matter of almost instant annihilation

As physical encounters go, the meeting of matter and antimatter ranks as one of the most decisive. When these opposites collide, they destroy each other. In a fraction of a second, their mass is converted into an enormous burst of energy.

23

How Are Fossils Dated?

Archaeologists determine the ages of bones and pre-
historic artifacts through a technique called radiocarbon dating. Taking a small sample of the item to be
dated, they measure how much of the radioactive isotope carbon 14 it contains. (Isotopes are two or more
forms of the same element that have either more or
fewer neutrons than normal atoms of the element; in
the case of carbon 14, eight neutrons rather than the
usual six.) Plants absorb carbon 14 from the air during
the food-producing activity of photosynthesis, and
herbivorous, or plant-eating, animals then acquire the
substance. When a plant or animal dies, its stores of
carbon 14 diminish because, like all radioactive elements, carbon 14 decays, losing about half its mass in
a span of 5,568 years, a period termed its half-life. By
comparing the amount of carbon 14 in a modern
antelope bone or a wooden tool with that in
their fossil counterparts, and knowing the
rate of carbon-14 decay, researchers can
calculate with fair accuracy when the
ancient antelope died or the tree from
which the tool was made was felled.
The older the fossil, the less carbon 14 it contains.

Radiocarbon dating

Proton

Beta particle

● **Carbon becomes nitrogen**

As a carbon-14 atom decays
into nitrogen 14, a neutron
splits into a proton, which is
kept, and an electron, which is
emitted as a beta particle.

Nitrogen 14

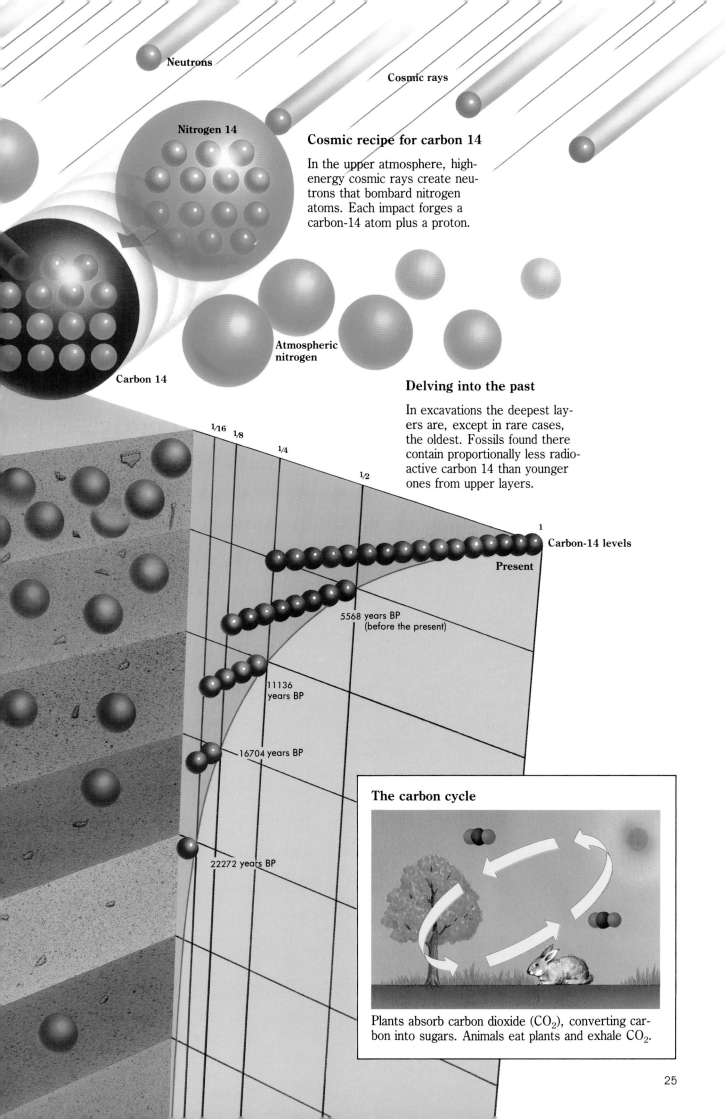

Neutrons

Cosmic rays

Nitrogen 14

Cosmic recipe for carbon 14

In the upper atmosphere, high-energy cosmic rays create neutrons that bombard nitrogen atoms. Each impact forges a carbon-14 atom plus a proton.

Atmospheric nitrogen

Carbon 14

Delving into the past

In excavations the deepest layers are, except in rare cases, the oldest. Fossils found there contain proportionally less radioactive carbon 14 than younger ones from upper layers.

1/16 1/8

1/4

1/2

1

Carbon-14 levels

Present

5568 years BP
(before the present)

11136
years BP

16704 years BP

22272 years BP

The carbon cycle

Plants absorb carbon dioxide (CO_2), converting carbon into sugars. Animals eat plants and exhale CO_2.

What Is the Nitrogen Cycle?

Whether it is in the atmosphere, land, or waters, nitrogen is often involved in chemical reactions. Factories and volcanoes spew out nitrogen, which is fixed, or converted into usable form by interaction with sunlight and lightning. Rain brings nitrogen back to Earth. Nitrogen, essential to life, is used to form amino acids to build protein. Plants and animals ingest and excrete nitrogen. Other nitrogen compounds wash into rivers and oceans, where they go through further chemical changes. Together, these events make up the nitrogen cycle.

A cycle of use and change

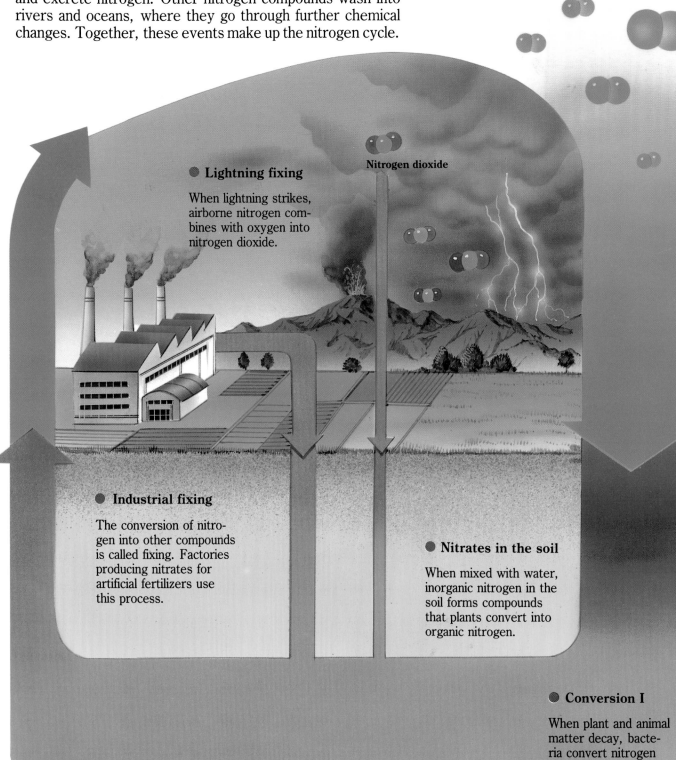

Nitrogen molecules

Nitrogen dioxide

● **Lightning fixing**

When lightning strikes, airborne nitrogen combines with oxygen into nitrogen dioxide.

● **Industrial fixing**

The conversion of nitrogen into other compounds is called fixing. Factories producing nitrates for artificial fertilizers use this process.

● **Nitrates in the soil**

When mixed with water, inorganic nitrogen in the soil forms compounds that plants convert into organic nitrogen.

● **Conversion I**

When plant and animal matter decay, bacteria convert nitrogen compounds into ammonia, then to nitrites and nitrates.

An ongoing exchange

Most of Earth's nitrogen is locked up in its crust as shown in the chart at right. The remaining nitrogen cycles from the air to land, from land to the seas, and from the seas back into the atmosphere. While living organisms need nitrogen to survive, some nitrogen compounds released by industry cause acid rain, poisoning lakes and damaging trees.

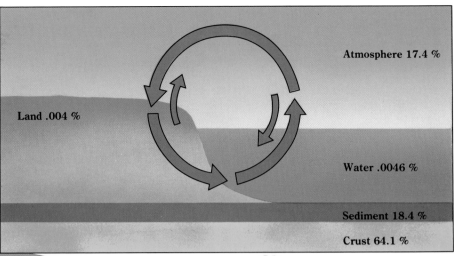

Atmosphere 17.4 %

Land .004 %

Water .0046 %

Sediment 18.4 %

Crust 64.1 %

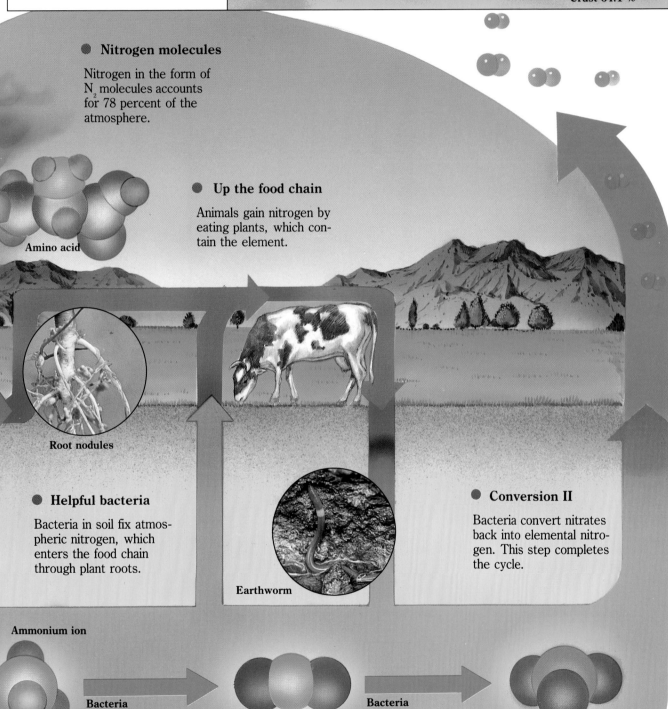

● Nitrogen molecules

Nitrogen in the form of N_2 molecules accounts for 78 percent of the atmosphere.

Amino acid

● Up the food chain

Animals gain nitrogen by eating plants, which contain the element.

Root nodules

● Helpful bacteria

Bacteria in soil fix atmospheric nitrogen, which enters the food chain through plant roots.

Earthworm

● Conversion II

Bacteria convert nitrates back into elemental nitrogen. This step completes the cycle.

Ammonium ion

Bacteria

Nitrite ion

Bacteria

Nitrate ion

Can Metal Bend?

Metals can be stretched, extruded as thin wires, or hammered or rolled flat without breaking. This flexibility comes from their basic structure. Metal atoms are arranged in neat ranks, with neighboring atoms sharing electrons. Because they are linked in this way, the atoms behave like a kind of mesh and readily reshape when subjected to outside stress or compression. Only when the outside force exceeds the ability of the atoms to respond will metals break. The properties of metal that allow it to be molded also make it an ideal industrial material.

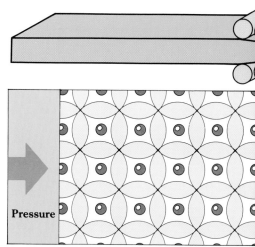

Closely packed metal atoms share electrons. The metal lattice bends in response to pressure, yet maintains strong bonds.

Shaping a beam

Heated aluminum is shaped into beams by a machine that pushes the metal through a die, in this case a perforated metal plate. The shape of the perforation determines what the cross section of the extruded metal looks like.

Molded beam

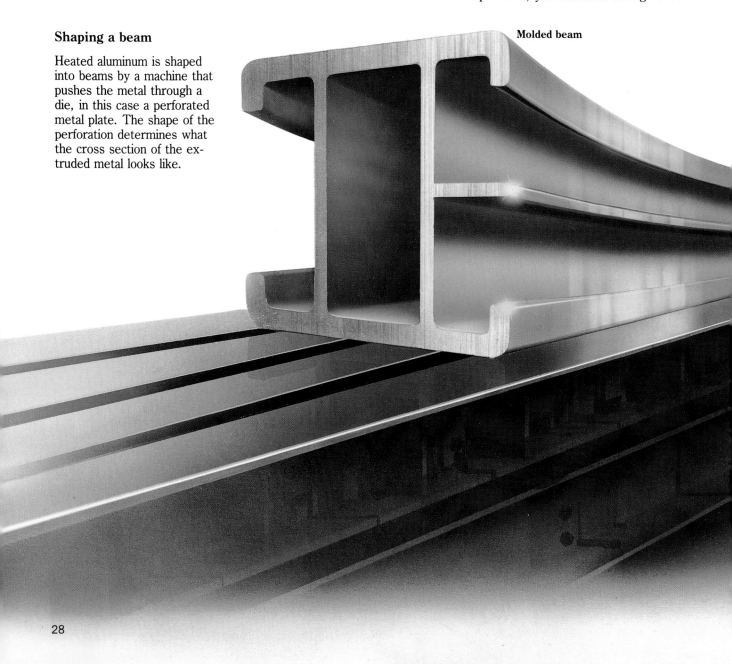

Making metal sheets

Graduated rollers apply pressure to a slab of metal, causing its atoms to slide across each other and rearrange their alignment, producing a thin, unbroken sheet of metal *(below)*.

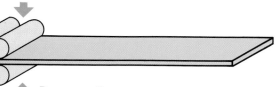

Pressure rollers

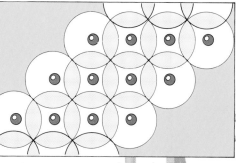

The atoms regroup and remain tied.

Leaves from solid gold

Gold is the most malleable of all metals. Two grams, or .07 ounce, of gold can be beaten into a 10-square-meter, or 107-square-foot, sheet of gold leaf that is .0001 millimeter, or .000004 inch, thick.

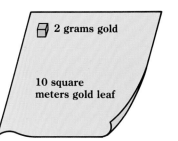

2 grams gold

10 square meters gold leaf

Shaping aluminum

High pressure applied by the stem *(far right)* forces heated aluminum through a die in the shape of a beam. Extrusion allows for the production of metal items that have complicated shapes and surfaces.

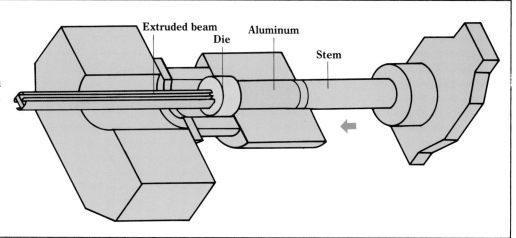

Extruded beam   Aluminum
            Die
                        Stem

What Makes Rubber Elastic?

Rubber can stretch, bend, and compress, then return to its original shape because of the way its molecules are organized. Rubber is a natural product extracted from certain kinds of trees. In its raw form, it is a colloid called latex, which is sticky and milky in color. When it is chemically treated with sulfur in a process called vulcanization, rubber molecules link in strands, or polymers, which are built up with atoms of carbon and hydrogen. These kinked, looping polymers are intertwined. Because the bonds between the molecules of the polymers allow for some motion, the tangled polymers flex and expand when they are subjected to outside forces. When the outside force is removed, the chemical bonds in the chains exert an opposite force that causes the rubber to rebound to its former shape.

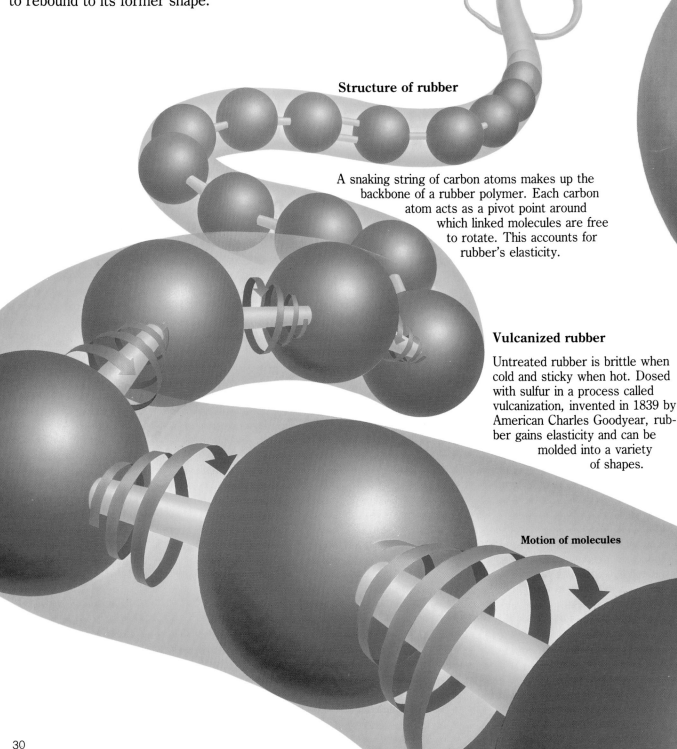

Structure of rubber

A snaking string of carbon atoms makes up the backbone of a rubber polymer. Each carbon atom acts as a pivot point around which linked molecules are free to rotate. This accounts for rubber's elasticity.

Vulcanized rubber

Untreated rubber is brittle when cold and sticky when hot. Dosed with sulfur in a process called vulcanization, invented in 1839 by American Charles Goodyear, rubber gains elasticity and can be molded into a variety of shapes.

Motion of molecules

30

Inside a rubber balloon

When air is blown into a balloon, the rubber stretches, and the tangled rubber molecules straighten out. Cross-links between molecules, bridged by sulfur atoms, strengthen the structure.

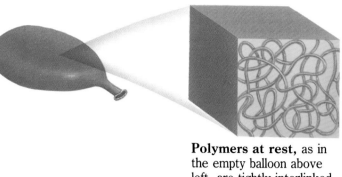

Polymers at rest, as in the empty balloon above left, are tightly interlinked.

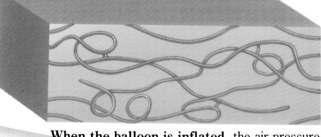

When the balloon is inflated, the air pressure inside causes the rubber polymers to stretch.

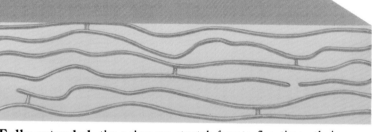

Fully extended, the polymers stretch four to five times their resting length. When all the pressure stops, the polymers will recoil to their original twisted shapes.

Lattice versus chain

Metal atoms in their orderly lattices *(top left)* rearrange themselves under pressure but beyond a certain limit will not bounce back. Chains of rubber molecules, though, return to their old shape.

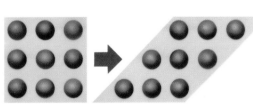

Metal atoms shift, then stay put.

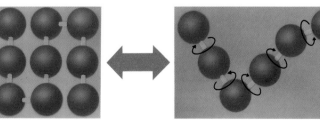

Rubber atoms shift, then rebound.

2
Changes in Matter

Many everyday events involve unseen changes in the relationships of the molecules and atoms that make up matter. Wet clothing on a clothesline dries. Ice melts to become water. Water boils and turns into steam. In every case, the structure of ordinary water molecules, each consisting of two atoms of hydrogen and one atom of oxygen, is arranged differently in a process known as a phase change. Depending on conditions such as temperature and pressure, water and other forms of matter may exist as a solid, a liquid, or a gas. Changes in any of these conditions may alter the form and properties of a substance. For example, at sea level water turns to steam at a temperature of 100° C., or 212° F. But at high altitudes, where there is less atmospheric pressure, water boils at a lower temperature. Other substances go through phase changes at different temperatures and in different ways. At room temperature frozen carbon dioxide, also known as dry ice, changes directly from solid to gas without melting first in a process called sublimation. Yet carbon dioxide can be turned into a liquid if the pressure and temperature conditions are right. This chapter examines these and other changes in matter to provide a better understanding of the behavior of molecules and atoms.

Water has unique properties because of the way in which its molecules cling to each other. Heat loosens the bonds, changing ice into water and water into steam, shown here as the molecule H_2O, consisting of hydrogen *(pink)* and oxygen *(blue)*.

How Can Water Become Ice or Steam?

Of all the substances on Earth, only water can assume all states of matter under natural conditions, that is, as a gas, a liquid, or a solid. But no matter which state water is in, each of its molecules consists of one atom of oxygen and two atoms of hydrogen; only its molecular behavior changes. When water freezes, it becomes a solid. The water molecules line up with one another to form rigid structures giving ice a low density. The molecules cannot move freely because the intermolecular forces holding them together are greater than the kinetic energy available to propel them into motion. When the temperature rises to 0° C., or 32° F., the heat loosens the forces holding the molecules together, and the molecules slip freely past one another, flowing as a liquid. Although the molecules retain a weak intermolecular attachment, the kinetic energy supplied by the heat keeps the molecules in constant motion. If the temperature increases further, the movement of the molecules becomes even livelier. Finally, at 100° C., or 212° F., the kinetic energy completely overcomes the energy of the intermolecular forces, and the molecules break apart, escaping into the air. The liquid has become a gas. Water vapor, as with any gas, has the lowest density of any state of matter. If water is contained in a tight plastic bag, it will expand and break the bag when it turns into vapor. This happens because the volume of a gas is greater than the volume of the solid or liquid form of the same substance.

The three states of water

Temperature

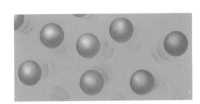

In the liquid state, water molecules *(blue balls)* cling loosely together, gliding freely around each other. The weakness of the intermolecular forces lets liquids flow.

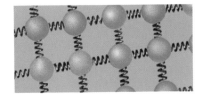

In ice, the intermolecular forces hold water molecules together in a rigid pattern. These molecules retain their structure at temperatures below 0° C., or 32° F.

Liquid

Solid

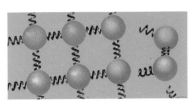

0° C./32° F.

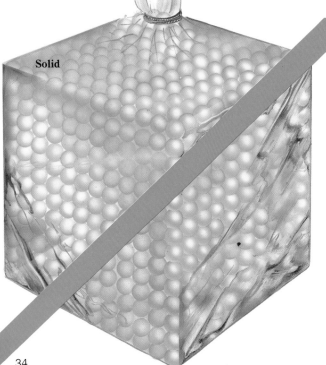

When ice begins to melt, above 0° C., or 32° F., the increase in kinetic energy overcomes the hold of the intermolecular forces, and the molecules loosen. The ice turns back into water.

Time ➡

34

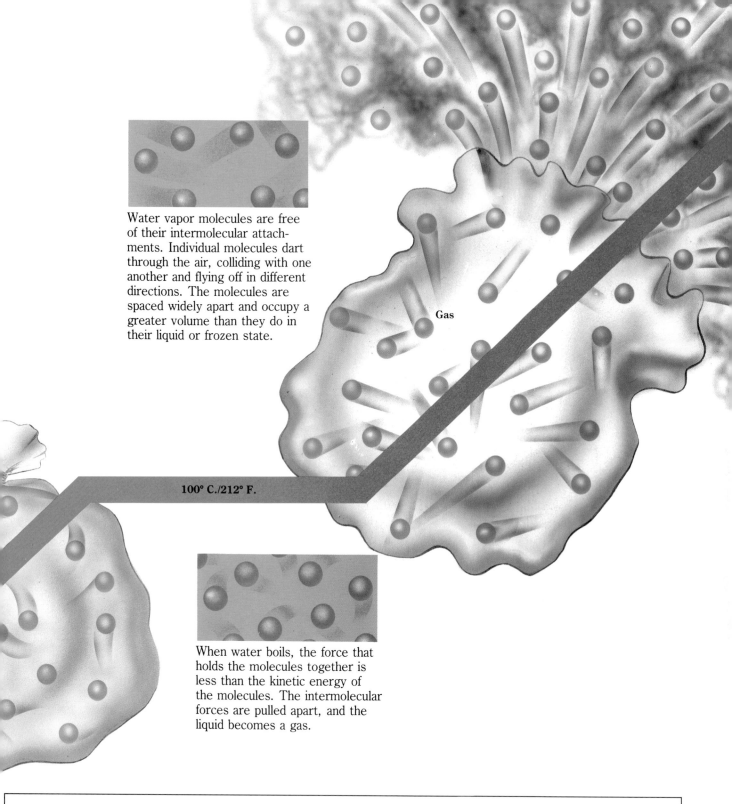

Water vapor molecules are free of their intermolecular attachments. Individual molecules dart through the air, colliding with one another and flying off in different directions. The molecules are spaced widely apart and occupy a greater volume than they do in their liquid or frozen state.

Gas

100° C./212° F.

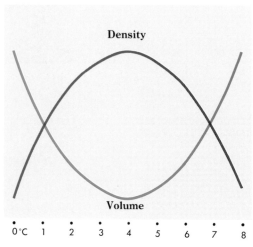

When water boils, the force that holds the molecules together is less than the kinetic energy of the molecules. The intermolecular forces are pulled apart, and the liquid becomes a gas.

Freezing and volume

Water is densest at 4° C., or 39° F. Between 4° C. and 0° C., or 32° F., the molecules begin to join; at 0° C., they form a tight pattern *(far right)* and become ice. Because of their shape, water molecules bunch closer together when they are loosely linked, as in a liquid, than when they are tight, as in ice; this makes them denser in liquids.

Density

Volume

0°C 1 2 3 4 5 6 7 8

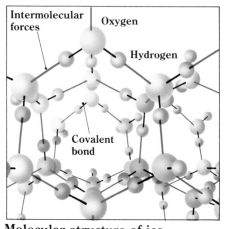

Intermolecular forces
Oxygen
Hydrogen
Covalent bond

Molecular structure of ice

Where Does Oxygen Come From?

Earth's atmosphere today contains about 21 percent oxygen and 78 percent nitrogen with traces of other gases. Early in Earth's history, the atmosphere contained no oxygen but was rich in nitrogen, carbon dioxide, ammonia, methane, and hydrogen sulfide. That began to change about three billion years ago, when the first living organisms appeared. Among the first life forms were simple blue-green algae, which through the process of photosynthesis obtained energy from the sun. The algae absorbed carbon dioxide from the atmosphere and chemically converted it into nutrients, releasing oxygen as a by-product. Over time the simple life forms developed into more complex plants that also produced oxygen; new creatures that needed oxygen to breathe also evolved, keeping everything in balance.

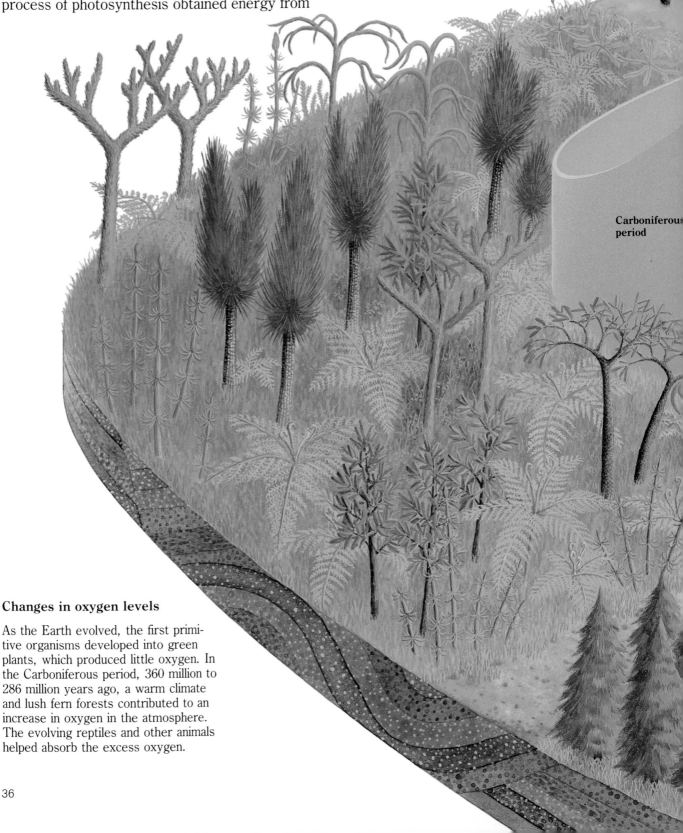

Carboniferous period

Changes in oxygen levels

As the Earth evolved, the first primitive organisms developed into green plants, which produced little oxygen. In the Carboniferous period, 360 million to 286 million years ago, a warm climate and lush fern forests contributed to an increase in oxygen in the atmosphere. The evolving reptiles and other animals helped absorb the excess oxygen.

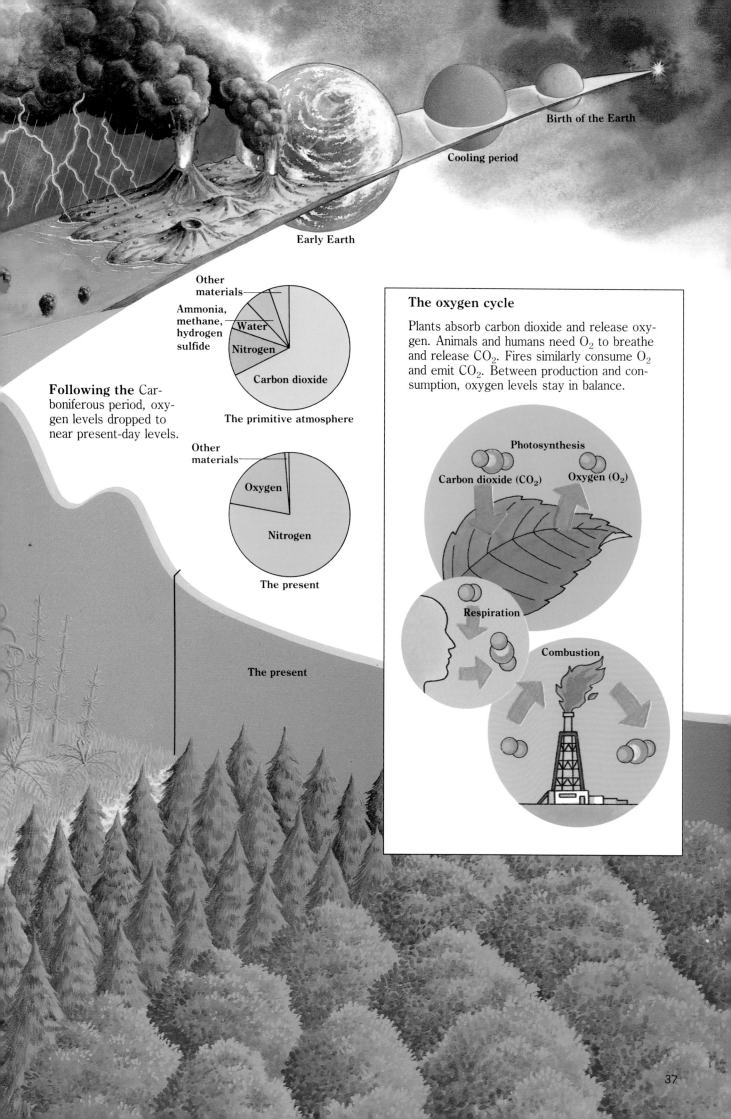

Birth of the Earth

Cooling period

Early Earth

Other materials

Ammonia, methane, hydrogen sulfide

Water

Nitrogen

Carbon dioxide

The primitive atmosphere

Following the Carboniferous period, oxygen levels dropped to near present-day levels.

Other materials

Oxygen

Nitrogen

The present

The present

The oxygen cycle

Plants absorb carbon dioxide and release oxygen. Animals and humans need O_2 to breathe and release CO_2. Fires similarly consume O_2 and emit CO_2. Between production and consumption, oxygen levels stay in balance.

Photosynthesis

Carbon dioxide (CO_2)   Oxygen (O_2)

Respiration

Combustion

Why Doesn't Dry Ice Melt?

At sea level, where atmospheric pressure is measured as 1 atmosphere, water comes to a boil at 100° C., or 212° F., and becomes a gas. At high altitudes, where there is less pressure, water boils at a lower temperature. Similarly, dry ice, or frozen carbon dioxide (CO_2), changes at 1 atmosphere and room temperature from a solid to a gas without melting first. Carbon dioxide is liquid only at more than 5.1 atmospheres, as in a fire extinguisher. When it is released into the air at 1 atmosphere, carbon dioxide becomes a gas. Pressure determines whether, at a given tem-

perature, a substance will be solid, liquid, or gas.

The diagrams below show what form a substance takes at particular combinations of temperature and pressure. Dividing lines show where phase changes occur. Two phases are said to be in equilibrium at their boundary. Along that line molecules can move from one phase to another without changing temperature. Where the solid-gas, solid-liquid, and liquid-gas boundaries meet is the triple point. All three states of matter are in equilibrium at this point and can be transformed into any other state.

Phase diagrams

Freezing point   Boiling point

Solid   Liquid   Gas

▲ Carbon dioxide at different pressures and temperatures

● **States of matter**

When carbon dioxide is under 20 atmospheres of pressure, as shown below and at left, it can exist as a solid, a liquid, or a gas, just as water can at 1 atmosphere of pressure.

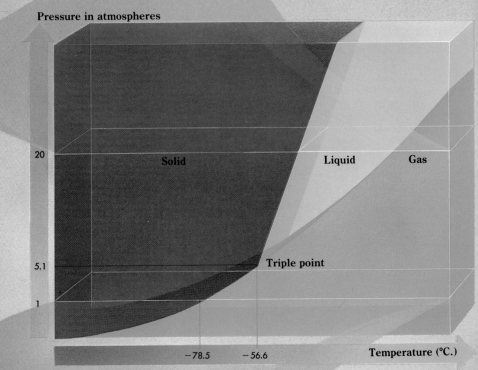

Pressure in atmospheres

● **Carbon dioxide at sea level**

At sea level (1 atmosphere), carbon dioxide can exist only as a solid or a gas. The change from solid to gas, or sublimation, begins at −78.5° C., or −109.3° F.; at room temperature, dry ice sublimes rapidly.

20   Solid   Liquid   Gas

5.1   Triple point

1

−78.5   −56.6   Temperature (°C.)

Dry ice

Solid   Gas

◄ **Changes in CO_2 at 1 atmosphere**

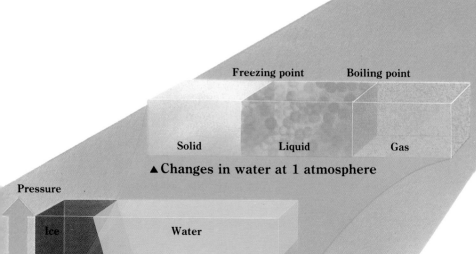

Freezing point · Boiling point

Solid · Liquid · Gas

▲ Changes in water at 1 atmosphere

Pressure

Ice · Water

1

0.006

Triple point · Water vapor

0 0.01 · 100 · Temperature (°C.)

● **Ice, water, and vapor**

At a pressure of 1 atmosphere, water can be solid, liquid, or gas. The phase diagram above shows the temperatures at which changes occur. At 0° C., or 32° F., water changes from solid to liquid; at 100° C., or 212° F., from liquid to gas. At low atmospheric pressure, water transforms from a solid to a gas.

The three states of matter

Matter can exist in three states. In changing from one state to another, it goes through melting (solid to liquid), solidification (liquid to solid), vaporization (liquid to gas), condensation (gas to liquid), sublimation (solid to gas), or condensation (gas to solid).

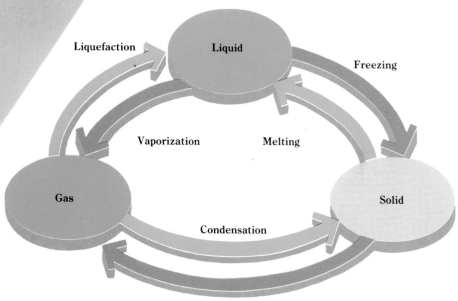

Liquefaction · Liquid · Freezing

Vaporization · Melting

Gas · Solid

Condensation

Sublimation

Dry ice, or frozen carbon dioxide, sublimes at room temperature to form a colorless gas.

At temperatures below 0° C., or 32° F., water vapor condenses to form ice crystals, or frost.

At low temperatures and pressures, water vapor condenses into water droplets or ice crystals to form clouds.

Can Salt Keep Water from Freezing?

Every winter freshwater lakes and streams freeze, while the saltwater oceans remain liquid, except in the coldest polar regions. Part of the reason for this phenomenon is that pure water freezes at 0° C., or 32° F., but salt water freezes more slowly, at −18° C., or 0° F.

When salt is dissolved in water, sodium and chloride ions *(pages 18-19)* attach themselves to some of the water molecules. These ions take up additional space and keep the crystalline lattice of ice from forming as it would in pure water. The ions also interact with the water molecules and disrupt the connections that hold the molecules together. The energy required to break these intermolecular forces removes heat from the water molecules, thereby lowering the temperature of the water. Eventually a new balance, or equi-

librium, is reached, and heat no longer flows away from the water molecules. For example, if 33 grams, or 1.16 ounces, of salt are mixed with 100 grams, or 3.5 ounces, of ice, equilibrium is reached at a temperature of −21.2° C., or −6.16° F., and the liquid freezes at that point. Salt and other substances that reduce the freezing point of matter are known as cryogens.

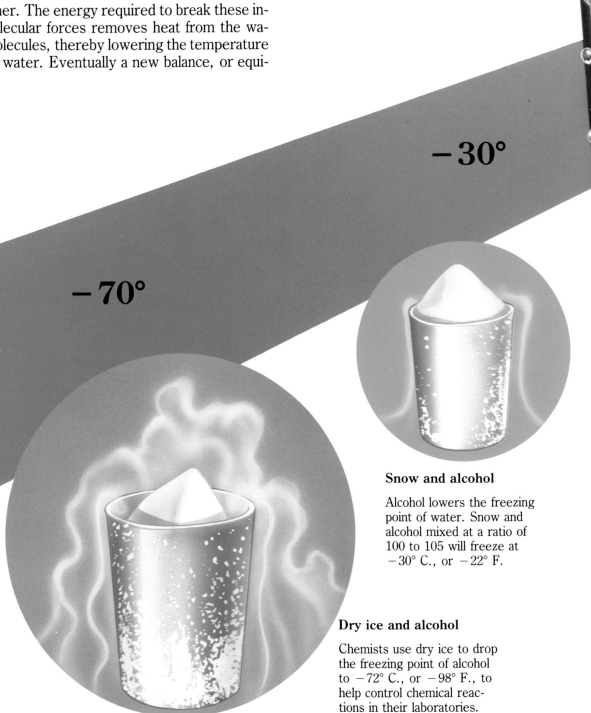

−30°

−70°

Snow and alcohol

Alcohol lowers the freezing point of water. Snow and alcohol mixed at a ratio of 100 to 105 will freeze at −30° C., or −22° F.

Dry ice and alcohol

Chemists use dry ice to drop the freezing point of alcohol to −72° C., or −98° F., to help control chemical reactions in their laboratories.

The reaction between sodium and chloride ions and water lowers the freezing point of the water.

Salt crystals
(sodium chloride)

Lowering the freezing point

0° C.

−20°

Ice melts
at 0° C., or 32° F.

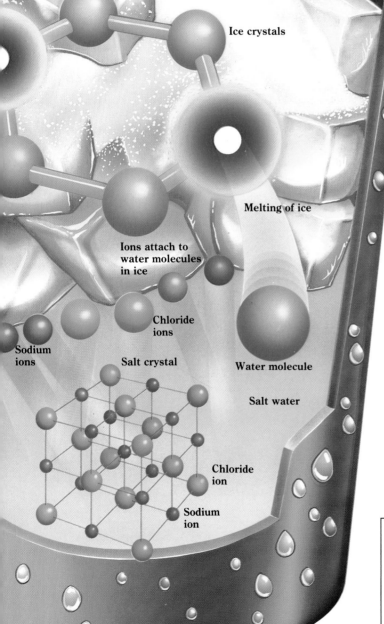

Ice crystals

Melting of ice

Ions attach to
water molecules
in ice

Chloride
ions

Sodium
ions

Salt crystal

Water molecule

Salt water

Chloride
ion

Sodium
ion

When ice melts

When salt is added to ice water, sodium and chloride separate, resulting in ions that attach to the water molecules. The ions break the intermolecular forces holding water molecules together, causing the molecules to break away from the ice crystals and the ice to melt. The energy, or heat, needed to break the intermolecular forces, called the heat of fusion, is drawn from the surrounding water. When salt is added to ice water, it takes 20 calories of heat per 1 gram, or 0.035 ounce, of solution to dissolve the salt. (A calorie is the amount of energy used to heat 1 gram of water by 10° C., or 50° F.) To melt 1 gram of ice, an additional 80 calories of heat are needed and drawn from the surrounding water, keeping the solution liquid and dropping its freezing point.

Melting agents

In winter, sodium chloride or calcium chloride is spread on roads and sidewalks to create a solution that keeps ice from forming, even at temperatures below 0° C., or 32° F.

Why Don't Oil and Water Mix?

When oil is poured on water, the oil rises to the top and does not mix with the water. A phenomenon called polarity causes these molecules to repel one another. In atoms, the positive electrical charge of the nucleus is balanced by the negative charge of the electrons; as a result, atoms have no net electrical charge. But in molecules, formed when atoms link up, one end of the molecule may have a positive charge and the other a negative charge, resulting in an unequal charge. Molecules possessing this electrical imbalance are said to be polar; molecules with no such imbalance are called nonpolar. Water consists of polar molecules because the oxygen atom has a partial negative charge and the hydrogen atoms a partial positive charge. On the other hand, oil molecules, composed mainly of carbon and hydrogen, are nonpolar, because they have the same positive charge everywhere. Polar molecules mix together because their positive and negative regions attract one another. Nonpolar molecules also attract one another but not as strongly. When a polar and a nonpolar substance are mixed together, the mutual attraction of the polar molecules squeezes out the nonpolar molecules, which are also drawn to one another. The two substances remain separate.

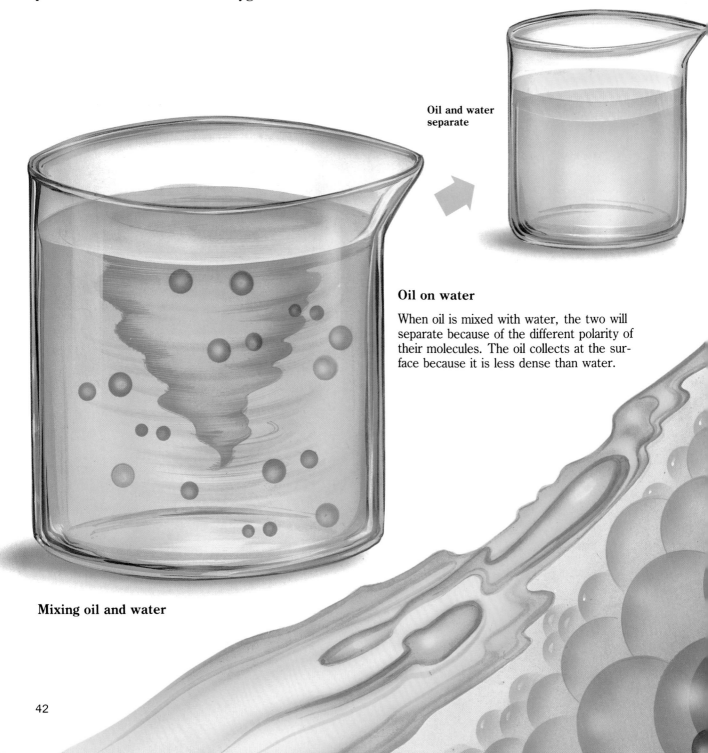

Oil and water separate

Oil on water

When oil is mixed with water, the two will separate because of the different polarity of their molecules. The oil collects at the surface because it is less dense than water.

Mixing oil and water

Substances in water

When ionic solids such as salt dissolve in water *(near right)*, their crystals separate into positive and negative ions, which are surrounded by water molecules. Ethanol *(far right)* combines with water because its molecules, like water's, are polar.

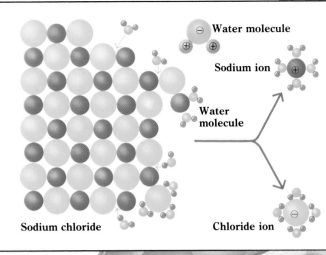

Sodium chloride

Water molecule

Sodium ion

Water molecule

Chloride ion

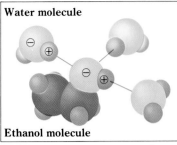

Water molecule

Ethanol molecule

A positive ethanol pole bonds to a negative water pole.

Salt dissolves in water, creating positive sodium ions and negative chloride ions.

Oil molecules

Oxygen atom

In water molecules, oxygen atoms, with a partial negative charge, attract the hydrogen atoms of other molecules, which have a partial positive charge.

Hydrogen atom

43

Why Are Most Elements Solid?

Of the 109 known elements, 92 occur naturally on Earth, and more than 80 percent of these appear in solid form. Although a few elements, such as oxygen, exist here as gas, and two, mercury and bromine, appear as a liquid, most are solid because of the temperature and pressure conditions on this planet. The average surface temperature on Earth is 15° C., or 59° F., and the melting point of most elements is at a higher temperature at a pressure of 1 atmosphere. On Venus, where the surface temperature is 500° C., or 900° F., many elements that would be solid on Earth are liquid. In the Sun, where the surface temperature of about 6,000° C., or 10,000° F., is higher than the boiling point of any element, all elements are in gaseous form. On the moons of Saturn, Uranus, and Neptune, the surface temperature is lower than −200° C., or −328° F., which is below the melting point of any element. That is why nitrogen appears as solid frost on some of those worlds rather than as gas as it does on Earth.

■ Solid, liquid, or gas

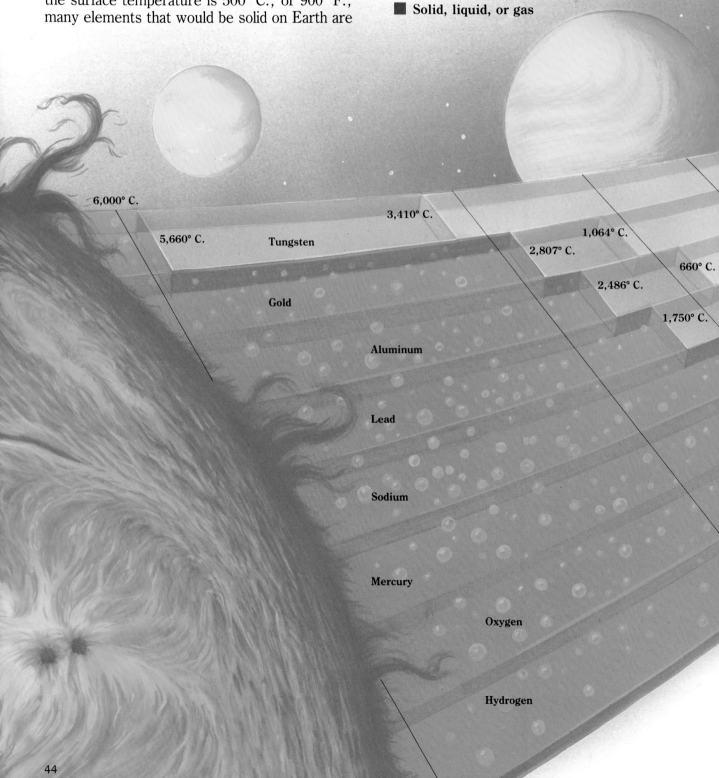

6,000° C.

3,410° C.

1,064° C.

5,660° C.   Tungsten

2,807° C.

660° C.

2,486° C.

Gold

1,750° C.

Aluminum

Lead

Sodium

Mercury

Oxygen

Hydrogen

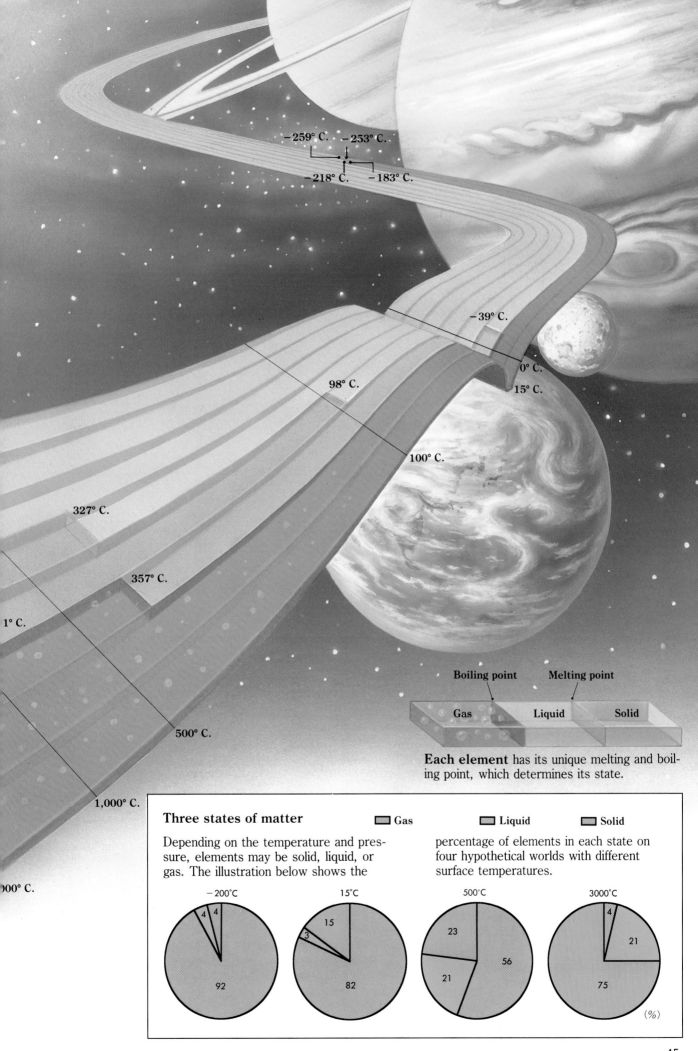

−259° C. −253° C.
−218° C. −183° C.

−39° C.

−0° C.

98° C. 15° C.

100° C.

327° C.

357° C.

1° C.

500° C.

1,000° C.

000° C.

Boiling point   Melting point

Gas   Liquid   Solid

Each element has its unique melting and boiling point, which determines its state.

Three states of matter
☐ Gas   ☐ Liquid   ☐ Solid

Depending on the temperature and pressure, elements may be solid, liquid, or gas. The illustration below shows the percentage of elements in each state on four hypothetical worlds with different surface temperatures.

−200°C
4 4
92

15°C
15
3
82

500°C
23
21
56

3000°C
4
21
75
(%)

45

Why Are Blimps Filled with Helium?

A ship floats in water because the weight of the volume of water it displaces is greater than the weight of the ship. Air is also considered a fluid, and an airship displaces a volume of air that weighs more than the airship. A volume of gas that is lighter than air therefore displaces a volume of air greater than its own weight. The difference between the weight of the gas in the blimp and the weight of the air it displaces is called buoyancy. The greater the difference, the greater the buoyancy. At a temperature of 0° C., or 32° F., and a pressure of 1 atmosphere, 1 liter, or 1.06 quarts, of air weighs 1.29 grams, or .04515 ounce. A liter of hydrogen, the lightest element, weighs just .09 gram, or .00315 ounce, and a liter of helium, the second-lightest gas, weighs .18 gram, or .0063 ounce. Hydrogen provides greater buoyancy but is highly flammable, therefore safe nonflammable helium is used in blimps. A helium-filled blimp displacing 6,666 cubic meters, or 235,376 cubic feet, of air would have a buoyancy equal to 7,400 kilograms, or 16,280 pounds. Assuming the blimp itself weighs 4,500 kilograms, or 9,900 pounds, it would then be capable of lifting a cargo weighing 2,900 kilograms, or 6,380 pounds.

Weight of 1 liter of gas

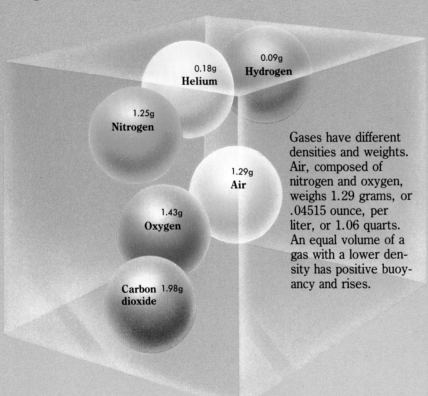

0.18g Helium

0.09g Hydrogen

1.25g Nitrogen

1.29g Air

1.43g Oxygen

Carbon dioxide 1.98g

Gases and buoyancy

Gases have different densities and weights. Air, composed of nitrogen and oxygen, weighs 1.29 grams, or .04515 ounce, per liter, or 1.06 quarts. An equal volume of a gas with a lower density has positive buoyancy and rises.

Controlling a blimp

In addition to helium, blimps contain separate cells filled with air. When air is added (1) or released (2) from the front or rear cells, the weight of the gases in the blimp increases or decreases, causing the blimp to descend or ascend. When all the air is released (3), the blimp will rise higher.

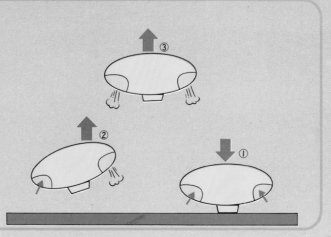

7400 kg

Buoyancy

Helium 6666 m³

Weight of the blimp

4500 kg

Buoyancy of a blimp

The buoyancy of a blimp is determined by the difference between its weight and the weight of the air it displaces. The greater the difference, the greater the weight the blimp can lift.

Weight of the load

2900 kg

How Does Soap Remove Dirt?

The simple act of washing one's hands or clothing in soap and water involves complicated chemical interactions at the molecular level. Typically, the dirt in clothes includes both dust from the air and greasy matter from the body. Because water is polar, that is, it has a small electrical charge *(pages 42-43)*, and oil is nonpolar, or has no charge, the two substances do not mix, and water alone cannot remove oily dirt. But the soap molecule has both a polar end, known as hydrophilic, or water-soluble, and a nonpolar hydro-

phobic, or nonsoluble, end. Working together, the two parts remove dirt. The nonpolar, hydrophobic ends in the soap molecules absorb, or cling to, the nonpolar oily dirt molecules. At the same time, the hydrophilic ends completely surround the oily dirt particles, forming spherelike structures called micelles. The surrounded dirt molecules are held in suspension in the water and prevented from reattaching themselves to the fabric. Rinsing away the soapy water removes the dirt molecules suspended in it.

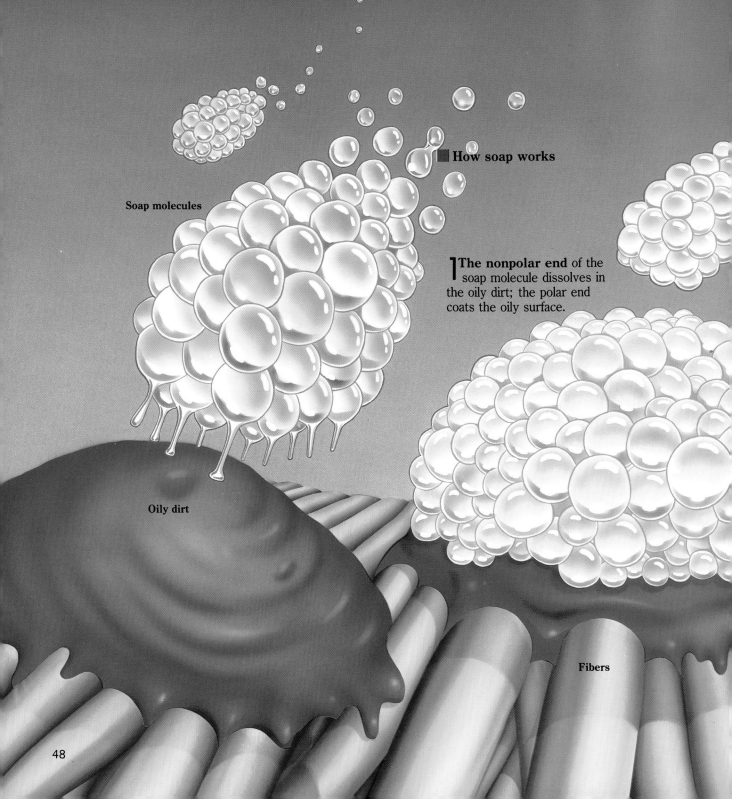

How soap works

Soap molecules

1 **The nonpolar end** of the soap molecule dissolves in the oily dirt; the polar end coats the oily surface.

Oily dirt

Fibers

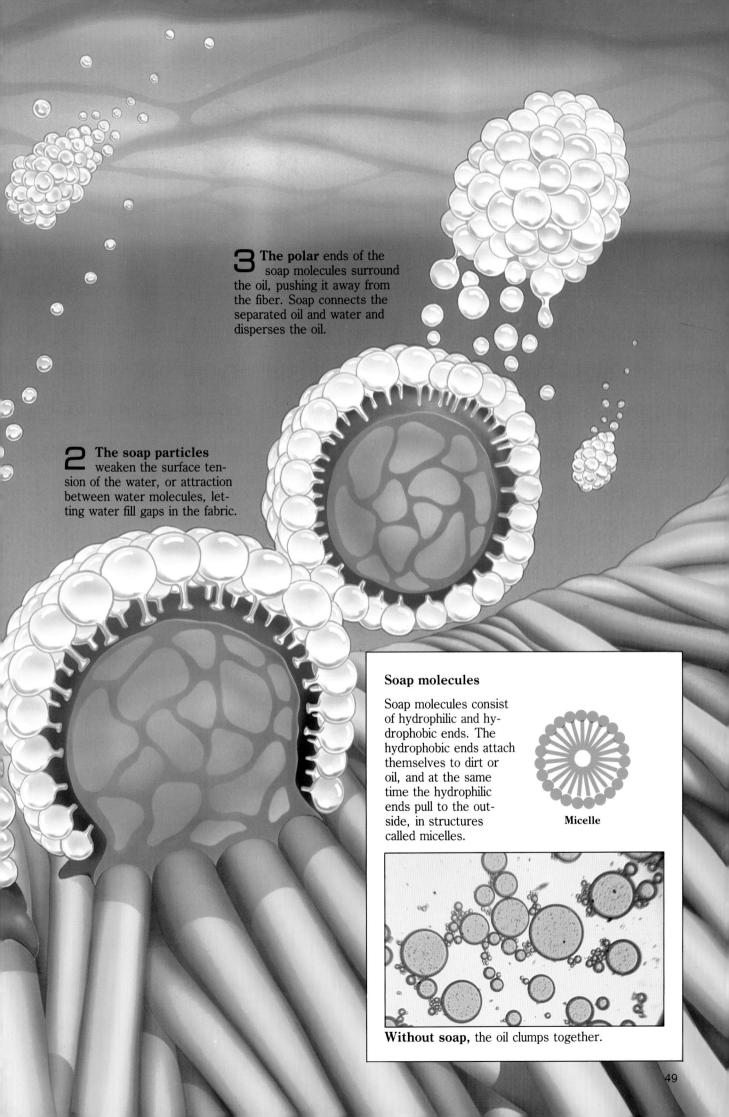

3 **The polar** ends of the soap molecules surround the oil, pushing it away from the fiber. Soap connects the separated oil and water and disperses the oil.

2 **The soap particles** weaken the surface tension of the water, or attraction between water molecules, letting water fill gaps in the fabric.

Soap molecules

Soap molecules consist of hydrophilic and hydrophobic ends. The hydrophobic ends attach themselves to dirt or oil, and at the same time the hydrophilic ends pull to the outside, in structures called micelles.

Micelle

Without soap, the oil clumps together.

How Do Fireworks Produce Colors?

Invented nearly 2,000 years ago in China, fireworks light up the night sky in spectacular displays. They are a colorful example of how electrons behave in the presence of excess energy, or heat. When a substance is heated by a black-gunpowder explosion, as in this case, the electrons of its atoms become excited and jump out of their stable orbits into new orbits with higher energy levels. But this state is unstable, and the electrons quickly return to their normal orbits. In the process, they release a burst of energy, or photons, in the form of visible light. This is the light that marks trails in the sky when fireworks explode. The color of the light depends on the composition of the fireworks. Each element packed in the shell releases light energy at unique wavelengths, each producing a specific color. In fireworks, sodium compounds are used to produce yellow light, strontium and lithium salts for red, copper for blue, and barium for green light. The combination of color and sound creates an exciting, multihued light show.

Sodium atom releasing light

Electron

Nucleus

Sodium atom

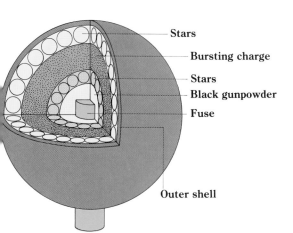

Stars
Bursting charge
Stars
Black gunpowder
Fuse

Outer shell

How fireworks burn

Firework shells contain a mixture of black gunpowder and compounds for producing light. A fuse ignites black-powder propellants that launch the shell into the air. Then a time-delay fuse sets off a bursting charge. As the powder burns, the pellets, or stars, of salt color the flames, creating bright patterns.

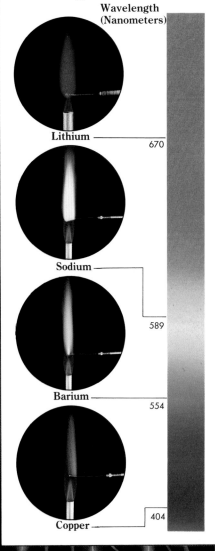

Color and wavelength

The color of fireworks depends on the substances they contain. As certain metals burn, each one produces a distinctive colored flame: red for lithium, yellow for sodium, green for barium, and blue for copper.

Wavelength
(Nanometers)

Lithium ——— 670

Sodium ——— 589

Barium ——— 554

Copper ——— 404

Electron dropping to normal orbit

Release of light

Excited electron

☐ Excited electrons

Heat energy causes electrons in an atom to jump into new orbits at a higher energy level. They quickly drop back to their normal orbits, emitting a burst of light at a specific wavelength. Here, a sodium atom emits yellow light.

How Can Bad Odors Be Removed?

Good or bad odors are caused by molecules released from the surface of various substances. A fresh fish will have hardly any smell at all, but bacteria on a decomposing fish will release strong odor molecules. The olfactory receptors in the nose will immediately detect even a few of these molecules. Odors can be eliminated physically, chemically, or biologically.

Removing odors physically can be accomplished with activated carbon filters, as in the refrigerator shown below. A tiny crystal of activated carbon contains countless holes, or pores, which give the crystal a large surface area relative to its volume. Odor molecules floating on air currents collide with the carbon particles and become trapped in these pores. Other agents that work in a similar way include silica gel and activated bauxite.

Odors can be chemically removed by using acids to neutralize alkaline odors and alkalines to neutralize acid odors. But only a limited number of substances can be treated chemically.

For biological odor removal, microorganisms are used to break down odor molecules, rendering them odorless. Biological agents are limited, however, by conditions such as temperature. Because of such limitations, activated carbon is the most effective means of odor removal.

Activated carbon

Activated carbon is made from organic materials such as coconut husks or animal bones, which are carbonized, or burned at high temperatures, and then steam-heated to between 800° and 1,000° C., or 1,470° and 1,830° F. This produces carbon crystals with a blistered surface, consisting of thousands of microscopic pores. Odor molecules are trapped in these pores and removed from the air.

Cross section of activated carbon

Odor molecules

Pores

Surface of activated carbon

If the surface of 1 gram, or 0.035 ounce, of activated carbon were spread out, it would cover some 2,000 square meters, or 21,500 square feet—about the area of a baseball field. At right, the photograph taken through a microscope shows activated carbon magnified 350 times. At this scale, the tiny pores look like craters on the Moon; each is capable of catching odor molecules.

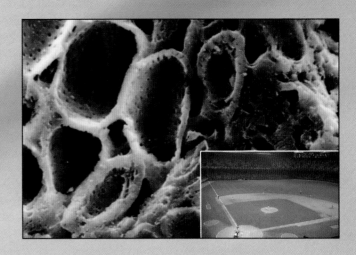

Activated carbon

Other methods for eliminating odors

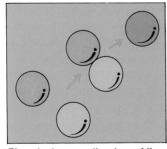

Chemical neutralization: Alkalines (*blue*) and acids (*pink*) cancel each other out.

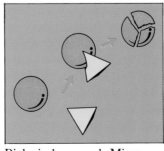

Biological removal: Microorganisms attack and break down odor molecules.

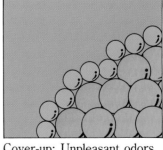

Cover-up: Unpleasant odors are masked by molecules producing pleasant odors.

3
Chemical Energy

When gasoline mixes with air and ignites, a rapid and violent transformation takes place. This chemical reaction produces carbon dioxide, water, and energy enough to power a car. Another group of chemical reactions changes the compound glucose into carbon dioxide and water. Although these reactions are less violent than the one involving gasoline, they produce enough energy to power the human body.

Countless different types of chemical reactions occur throughout the universe, and they all involve changing the composition of matter. This change consists of a regrouping of the atoms in one set of molecules and breaking the complex bonds that hold them together to produce a different arrangement. When iron rusts, for example, oxygen molecules react with iron atoms to form the new substance iron oxide. The atoms in iron oxide line up differently from those in either oxygen molecules or iron. Some reactions happen slowly and release only a small amount of energy. Other reactions require a separate source of energy before they can occur. In the series of chemical reactions known as photosynthesis, plants use the energy in sunlight to join together six molecules of carbon dioxide and six molecules of water to produce one molecule of glucose and six molecules of oxygen.

A rocket blasting into space requires a vast amount of energy to overcome gravity. That energy comes from the rapid chemical reaction that occurs when fuel is mixed with oxygen and is ignited in the rocket's engines.

Why Does Iron Rust?

In nature, iron usually exists in combination with other elements such as oxygen; its ore is known as iron oxide. Once the iron has been extracted from the ore and worked into steel, it reacts easily with other substances. When in contact with oxygen in water or air, iron will undergo an oxidation-reduction, or redox, reaction, and gradually return to its natural form of iron oxide. A redox reaction proceeds in two parts: oxidation, in which atoms lose electrons, and reduction, in which atoms gain electrons. If iron is exposed to water, as the ship's hull at right, oxygen atoms dissolved in the water will draw electrons away from iron atoms, resulting in positive iron ions (Fe^{2+}) that have an electrical charge. Oxygen atoms also react with water molecules (H_2O), which gain electrons and reduce an oxygen atom to form hydroxide ions (OH^-). The hydroxide ions, in turn, attach to the iron ions to produce iron hydroxide [$Fe(OH)_2$]. Additional dissolved oxygen slowly reacts with the iron hydroxide to form iron oxide, or rust (Fe_2O_3). Rust is a brittle substance that easily flakes off the surface to expose more iron atoms, and the process starts over again. Rust can be stopped by replacing the electrons that iron atoms lose by using sacrificial anodes or by applying a low-voltage electric current to the ship's hull at a point opposite to the redox reaction.

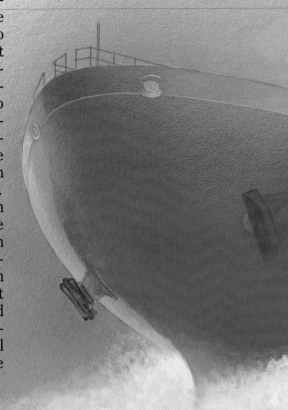

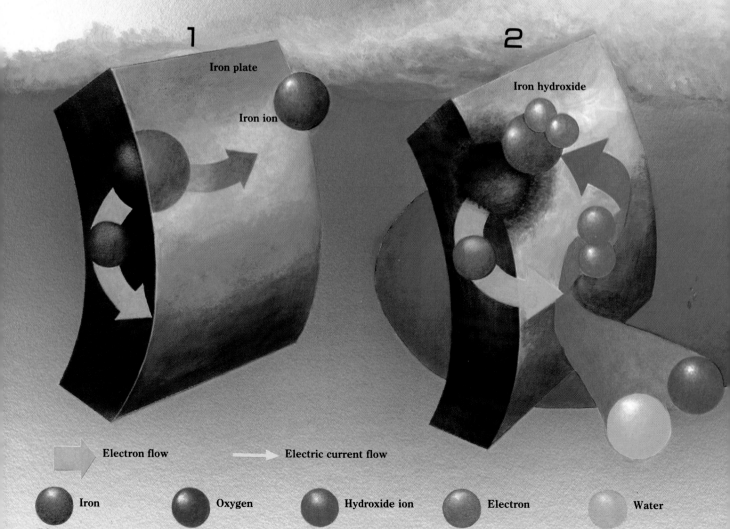

1

Iron plate

Iron ion

2

Iron hydroxide

Electron flow   Electric current flow

Iron   Oxygen   Hydroxide ion   Electron   Water

How things rust

1 **At the oxidation site,** or anode, iron atoms react with oxygen in the water, giving up two electrons and becoming positively charged iron ions.

2 **At the reduction site,** or cathode, H_2O gains electrons, splitting into hydrogen atoms (H) and negative hydroxide ions (OH^-), which react with iron ions.

3 **As the positively charged iron** ions react with the iron hydroxide ions, they form rust. The electron flow gives rise to a weak electric current.

From ore to iron to rust

When miners dig up iron ore, the iron is bound with oxygen as iron oxide. To obtain pure iron, the oxygen is removed in a blast furnace. It takes more than 2 tons of ore to make 1 ton of iron. Over time, the iron recombines with oxygen and begins to rust.

Iron ore   Rust-coated iron

Iron

Halting rust

Electron flow

3

Zinc

Iron plate

Anode

Cathode

− +

Attached to a ship, a zinc anode corrodes instead of the iron hull.

External power source

A low-voltage current passes through the ship's hull to replace lost electrons.

Sacrificial anode

Because zinc loses electrons faster than iron, it can act as a so-called sacrificial anode. In oxidation, zinc electrons replace lost iron electrons.

Zinc ion

Zinc

Iron plate

How Do Batteries Make Electricity?

Automobile batteries consist of electrochemical cells, which convert chemical energy to electrical energy. Inside the battery *(right),* negative plates, or anodes, made of lead (Pb) and positive plates, or cathodes, made of lead dioxide (PbO_2) are submerged in a sulfuric acid solution (H_2SO_4). As the turn of the ignition key closes a circuit, the battery produces electricity in an oxidation-reduction reaction. At the anode, lead atoms lose two electrons (e^-) and become positively charged lead ions (Pb^{2+}). The lead ions combine with the sulfate ions (SO_4^{2-}) in the sulfuric acid solution and produce lead sulfate ($PbSO_4$). At the cathode, lead dioxide (PbO_2) gains electrons, releasing oxygen, which attaches to hydrogen ions (H^+) to produce water and lead sulfate. As this reaction runs its course, the flow of electrons creates an electric current. The amount of lead sulfate and water increases, and the concentration of sulfuric acid and the amount of lead and lead dioxide decreases. When the reactants are depleted, the battery stops producing electricity. The reaction, however, can be reversed by recharging the battery.

The structure of a battery

A car's lead storage battery is made up of six cells, each with a negative and a positive terminal. A cell generates 2 volts of energy. Connected in series, the battery's six cells produce 12 volts.

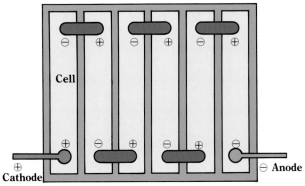

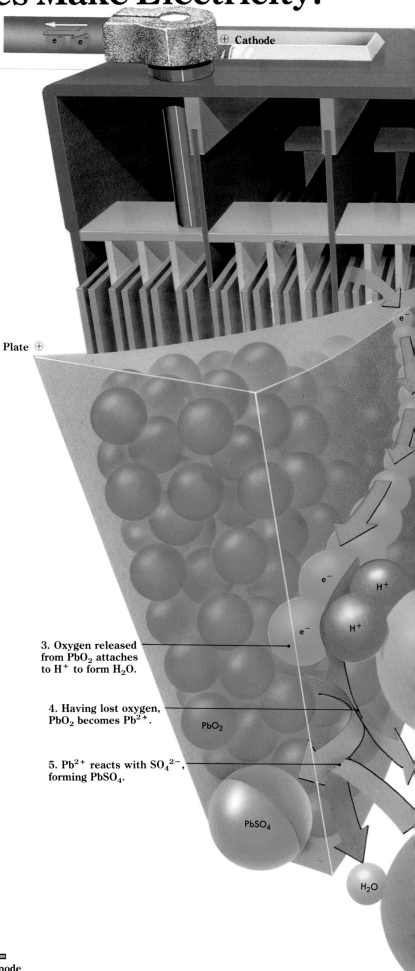

⊕ Cathode

Plate ⊕

e^-

e^- H^+

e^- H^+

3. Oxygen released from PbO_2 attaches to H^+ to form H_2O.

4. Having lost oxygen, PbO_2 becomes Pb^{2+}.

PbO_2

5. Pb^{2+} reacts with SO_4^{2-}, forming $PbSO_4$.

$PbSO_4$

H_2O

The chemistry of a battery

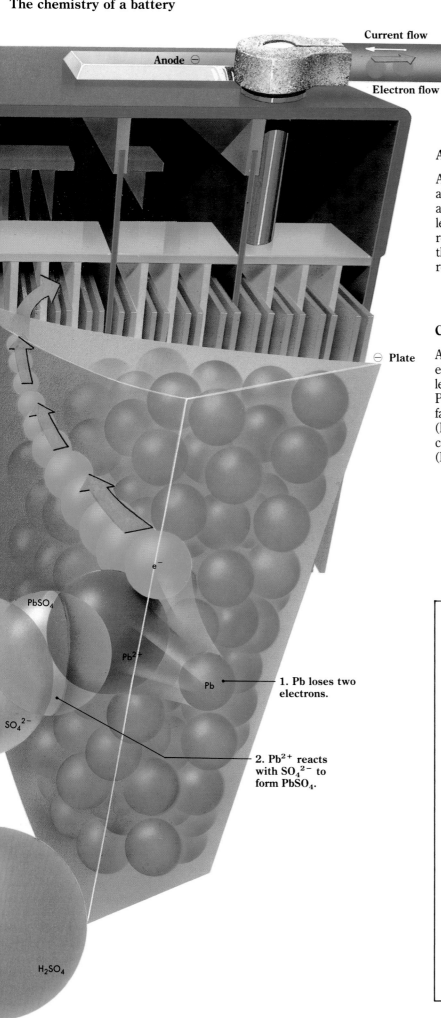

Current flow

Anode ⊖

Electron flow

⊖ Plate

PbSO₄

e⁻

Pb²⁺

SO₄²⁻

Pb

1. Pb loses two electrons.

2. Pb²⁺ reacts with SO₄²⁻ to form PbSO₄.

H₂SO₄

Anode reaction

At the anode *(above, left)*, lead atoms (Pb) give up two electrons and become positively charged lead ions (Pb^{2+}). The lead ions react with sulfate ions (SO_4^{2-}) in the sulfuric acid solution (H_2SO_4), resulting in lead sulfate ($PbSO_4$).

Cathode reaction

At the positive pole *(far left)*, electrons (e^-) reduce lead ions in lead oxide (PbO_2) from Pb^{4+} to Pb^{2+}, which combines with sulfate ions to produce lead sulfate ($PbSO_4$). The oxygen released combines with hydrogen ions (H^+) to produce water.

Charging a battery

By attaching an external power source to a battery, a current runs through the poles in the opposite direction from normal discharge. This changes the lead sulfate and water back into the original reactants: lead, lead dioxide, and sulfuric acid.

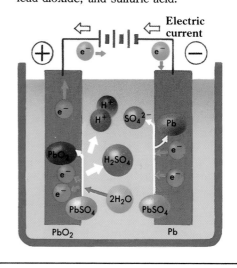

Electric current

⊕ ⊖

e⁻ e⁻

e⁻

H⁺
H⁺

SO₄²⁻ Pb

PbO₂ H₂SO₄ e⁻

e⁻

e⁻ 2H₂O

PbSO₄ PbSO₄

PbO₂ Pb

How Does a Car Engine Run?

The combustion of gasoline

1 Intake: On the intake stroke, the piston descends, pulling a mixture of air and vaporized gasoline through the open intake valve into the cylinder.

2 Compression: When the piston rises, it compresses the fuel-air mixture, which raises the temperature and pressure inside the cylinder.

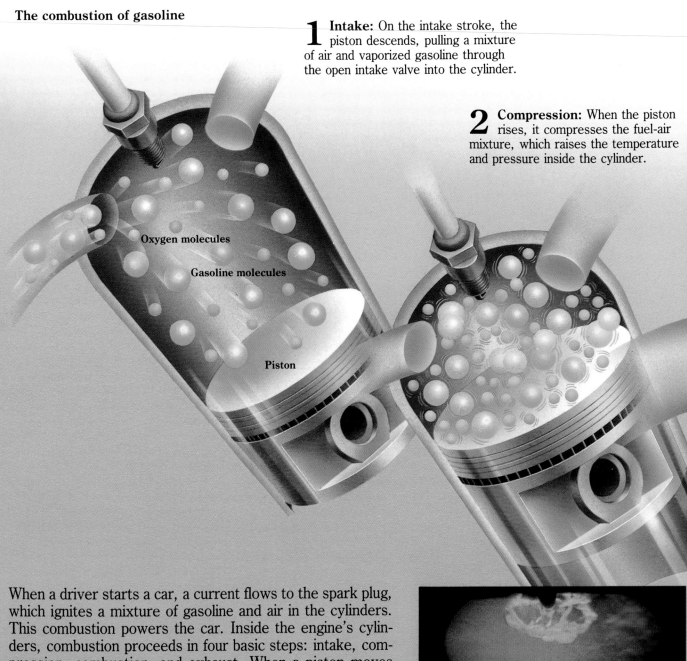

Oxygen molecules

Gasoline molecules

Piston

When a driver starts a car, a current flows to the spark plug, which ignites a mixture of gasoline and air in the cylinders. This combustion powers the car. Inside the engine's cylinders, combustion proceeds in four basic steps: intake, compression, combustion, and exhaust. When a piston moves down, the intake valve opens, and a mixture of air and vaporized gasoline is drawn into the cylinder. The intake valve closes as the piston rises again and compresses the mixture. The compression excites the gas molecules, raising the temperature to 393° C., or 740° F., or more. When the spark plug ignites the highly pressurized mixture, a controlled burn causes the gas to expand rapidly, forcing the piston down. In the fourth and final step, the exhaust valve opens as the piston rises, forcing the exhaust gases out of the cylinder and leaving the piston at the top of the cylinder ready to begin the next cycle. The piston's up-and-down motion transmits its power to several sets of gears, which turn the wheels.

In a diesel engine the compression ratio is much greater and a spark plug is not needed, as diesel fuel spontaneously combusts under the higher temperatures and pressures.

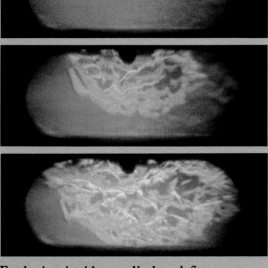

Explosion inside a cylinder: A flame spreads out from the initial combustion point.

Piston and crankshaft

Intake

The intake valve opens as the piston descends, letting in air and fuel.

Compression

The crankshaft turns and pushes the piston up, compressing the gas.

Combustion

A spark ignites the gasoline, which burns and forces the piston down.

Exhaust

The exhaust valve opens as the piston rises, expelling the exhaust gases.

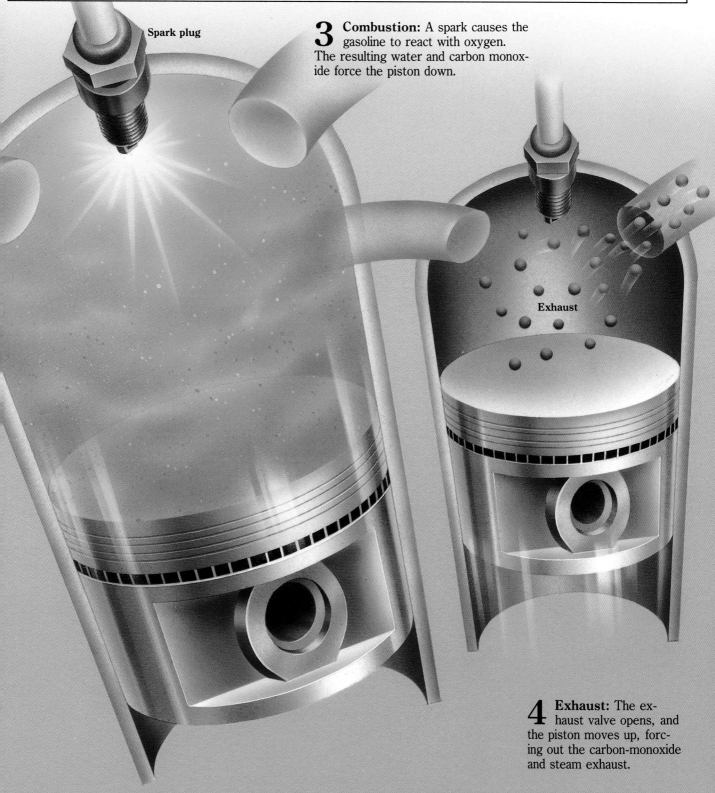

3 **Combustion:** A spark causes the gasoline to react with oxygen. The resulting water and carbon monoxide force the piston down.

Spark plug

Exhaust

4 **Exhaust:** The exhaust valve opens, and the piston moves up, forcing out the carbon-monoxide and steam exhaust.

How Can Bronze Become Silver?

Silver-plating

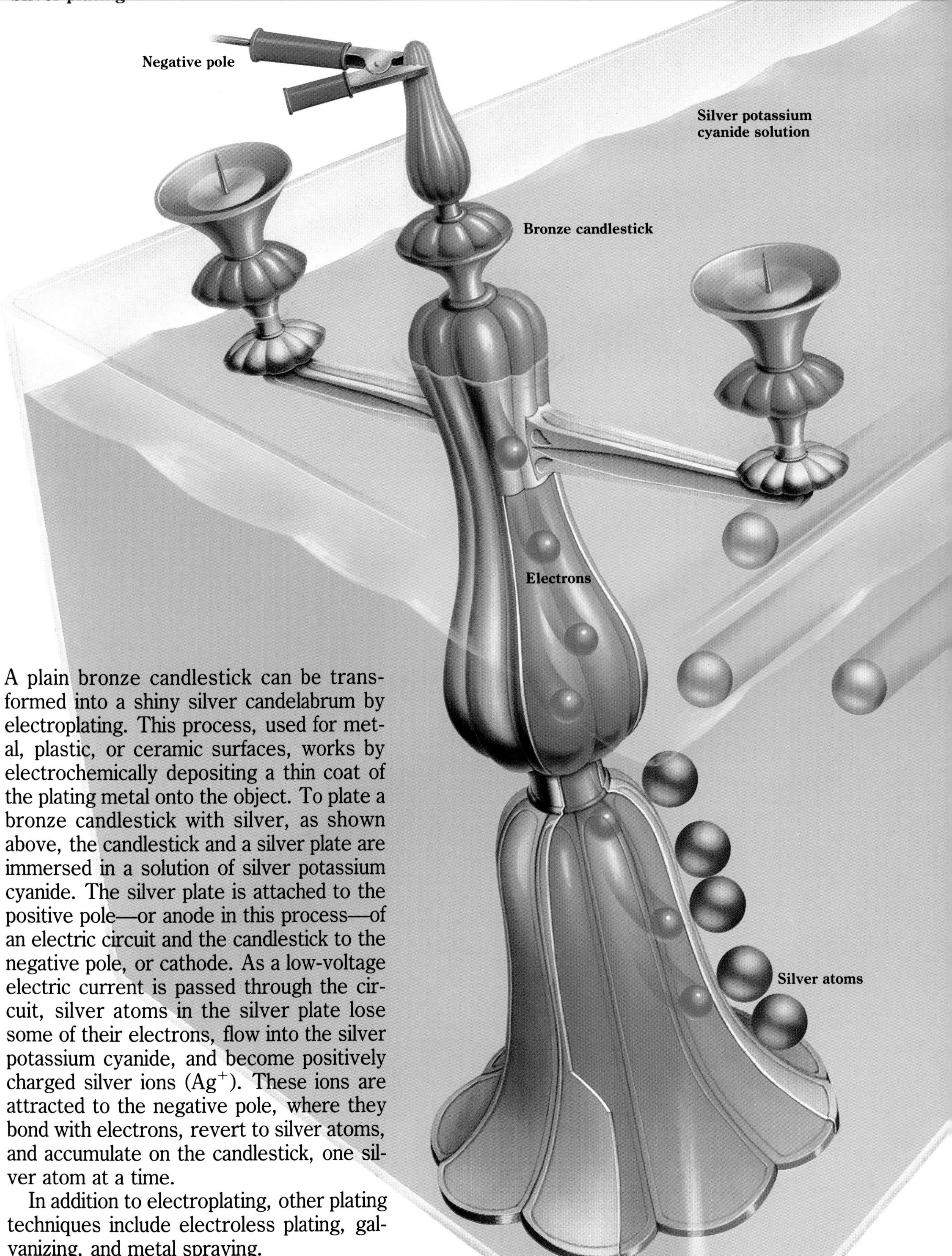

Negative pole

Silver potassium cyanide solution

Bronze candlestick

Electrons

Silver atoms

A plain bronze candlestick can be transformed into a shiny silver candelabrum by electroplating. This process, used for metal, plastic, or ceramic surfaces, works by electrochemically depositing a thin coat of the plating metal onto the object. To plate a bronze candlestick with silver, as shown above, the candlestick and a silver plate are immersed in a solution of silver potassium cyanide. The silver plate is attached to the positive pole—or anode in this process—of an electric circuit and the candlestick to the negative pole, or cathode. As a low-voltage electric current is passed through the circuit, silver atoms in the silver plate lose some of their electrons, flow into the silver potassium cyanide, and become positively charged silver ions (Ag^+). These ions are attracted to the negative pole, where they bond with electrons, revert to silver atoms, and accumulate on the candlestick, one silver atom at a time.

In addition to electroplating, other plating techniques include electroless plating, galvanizing, and metal spraying.

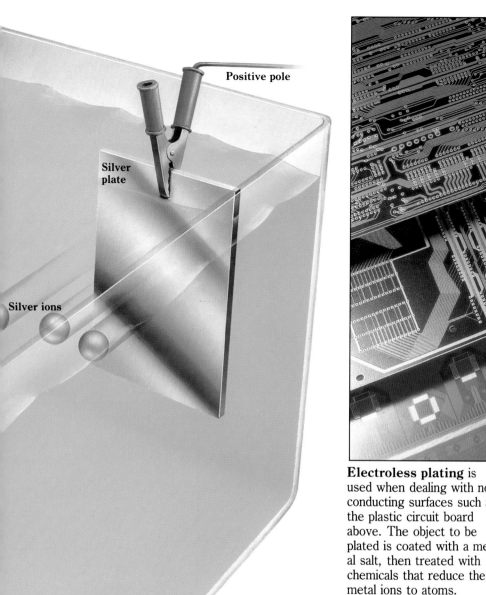

Positive pole

Silver plate

Silver ions

Electroless plating is used when dealing with non-conducting surfaces such as the plastic circuit board above. The object to be plated is coated with a metal salt, then treated with chemicals that reduce the metal ions to atoms.

The chemistry of electroplating

By sending an electric current through the positive pole at the silver plate, silver atoms lose electrons and combine with the silver potassium cyanide solution, becoming positively charged silver ions. The silver ions are attracted to the negative pole, where they gain electrons, depositing silver atoms onto the candlestick.

Other plating methods

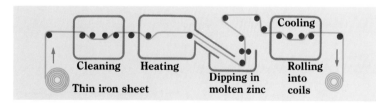

Cleaning   Heating   Dipping in molten zinc   Cooling   Rolling into coils

Thin iron sheet

Continuous hot dip galvanizing *(above)* plates zinc onto coil-fed iron or steel. The iron or steel is first cleaned and heated, then dipped into a bath of molten zinc so as to galvanize, or coat, the metal.

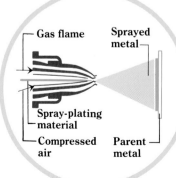

Gas flame   Sprayed metal

Spray-plating material

Compressed air   Parent metal

Metal spraying works by melting a thin wire or powder of the plating metal in a gas flame and spraying tiny bubbles of the metal onto the target object with compressed air.

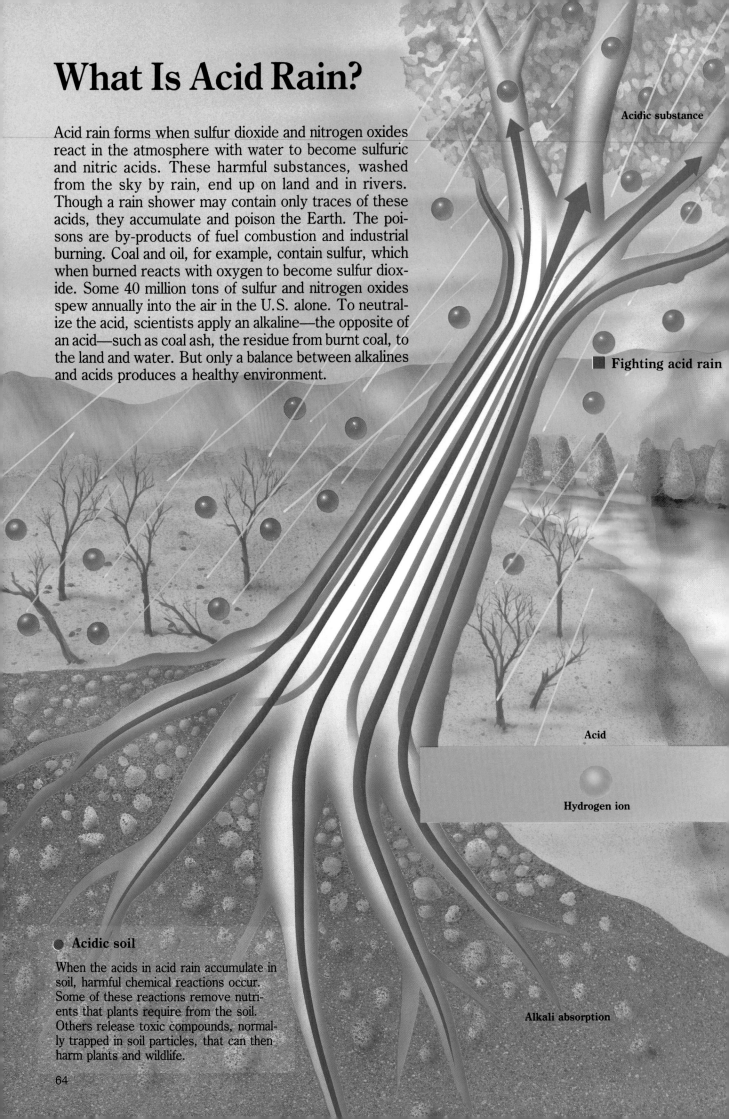

What Is Acid Rain?

Acid rain forms when sulfur dioxide and nitrogen oxides react in the atmosphere with water to become sulfuric and nitric acids. These harmful substances, washed from the sky by rain, end up on land and in rivers. Though a rain shower may contain only traces of these acids, they accumulate and poison the Earth. The poisons are by-products of fuel combustion and industrial burning. Coal and oil, for example, contain sulfur, which when burned reacts with oxygen to become sulfur dioxide. Some 40 million tons of sulfur and nitrogen oxides spew annually into the air in the U.S. alone. To neutralize the acid, scientists apply an alkaline—the opposite of an acid—such as coal ash, the residue from burnt coal, to the land and water. But only a balance between alkalines and acids produces a healthy environment.

Acidic substance

■ **Fighting acid rain**

Acid

Hydrogen ion

● **Acidic soil**

When the acids in acid rain accumulate in soil, harmful chemical reactions occur. Some of these reactions remove nutrients that plants require from the soil. Others release toxic compounds, normally trapped in soil particles, that can then harm plants and wildlife.

Alkali absorption

64

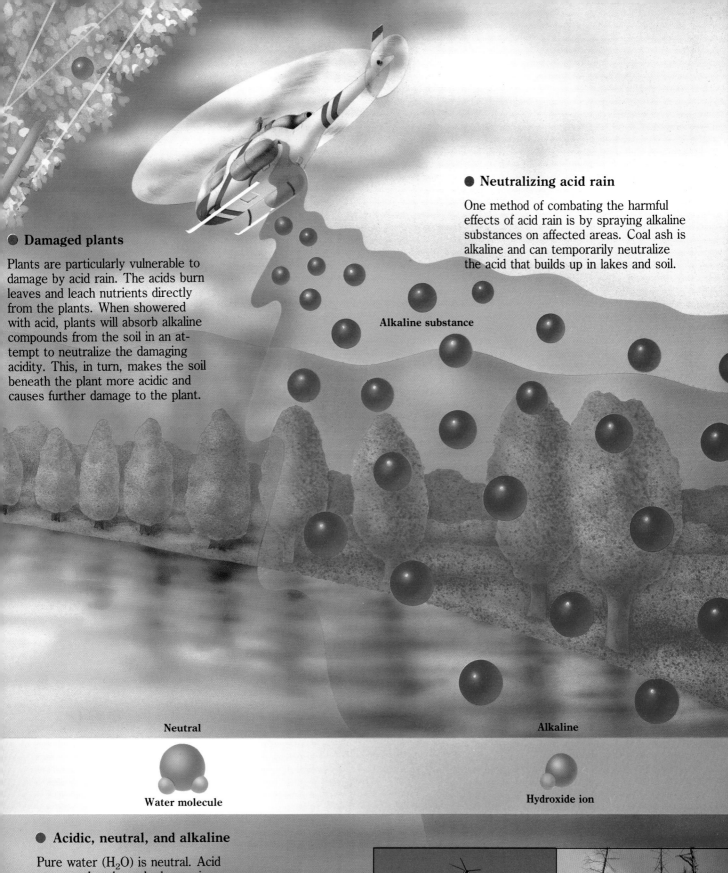

Damaged plants

Plants are particularly vulnerable to damage by acid rain. The acids burn leaves and leach nutrients directly from the plants. When showered with acid, plants will absorb alkaline compounds from the soil in an attempt to neutralize the damaging acidity. This, in turn, makes the soil beneath the plant more acidic and causes further damage to the plant.

Neutralizing acid rain

One method of combating the harmful effects of acid rain is by spraying alkaline substances on affected areas. Coal ash is alkaline and can temporarily neutralize the acid that builds up in lakes and soil.

Alkaline substance

Neutral

Alkaline

Water molecule

Hydroxide ion

Acidic, neutral, and alkaline

Pure water (H_2O) is neutral. Acid compounds release hydrogen ions (H^+), while alkaline substances generate hydroxide ions (OH^-). Combining the two—one hydrogen ion and one hydroxide ion—produces water. Thus adding enough of an alkaline substance can neutralize excess acid, returning the soil or water to a condition close to neutral.

Spraying to neutralize acids keeps a forest alive.

Why Do Things Burn?

A lump of coal left alone will remain unchanged for millions of years. But as soon as that piece of coal is added to a fire, it receives the spark necessary to activate its energy and begins to burn. In the high heat of the flames, oxygen reacts with the molecules in coal—and other substances—and breaks the chemical bonds holding those molecules together. The energy that is stored in these bonds produces the heat and light of fire. The chemical reactions are called combustion and occur rapidly, releasing so much heat that a burning substance grows hotter as combustion proceeds, but eventually combustion consumes all the high-energy molecules present and the fire goes out.

Photosynthesis and combustion

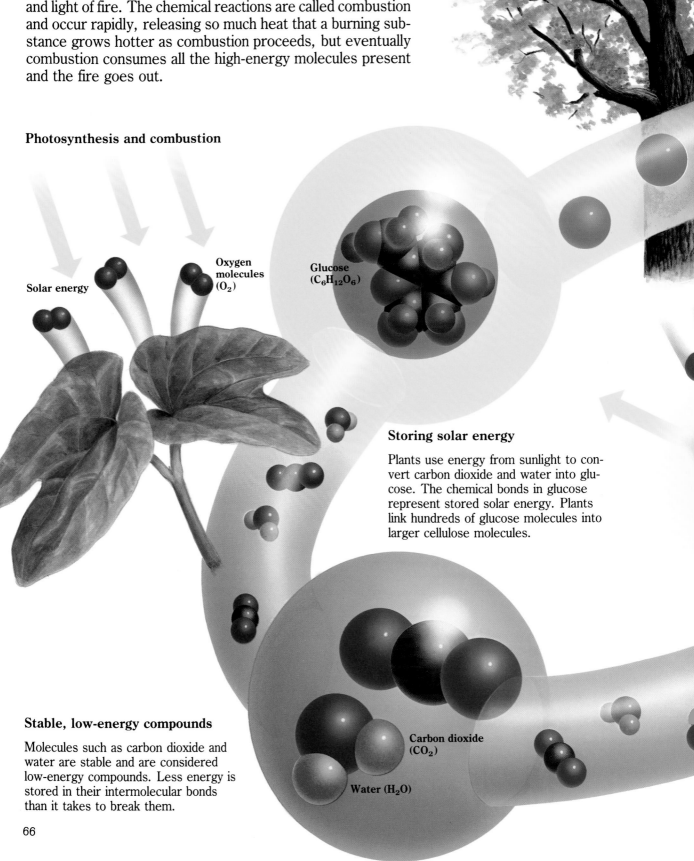

Solar energy

Oxygen molecules (O_2)

Glucose ($C_6H_{12}O_6$)

Storing solar energy

Plants use energy from sunlight to convert carbon dioxide and water into glucose. The chemical bonds in glucose represent stored solar energy. Plants link hundreds of glucose molecules into larger cellulose molecules.

Stable, low-energy compounds

Molecules such as carbon dioxide and water are stable and are considered low-energy compounds. Less energy is stored in their intermolecular bonds than it takes to break them.

Carbon dioxide (CO_2)

Water (H_2O)

66

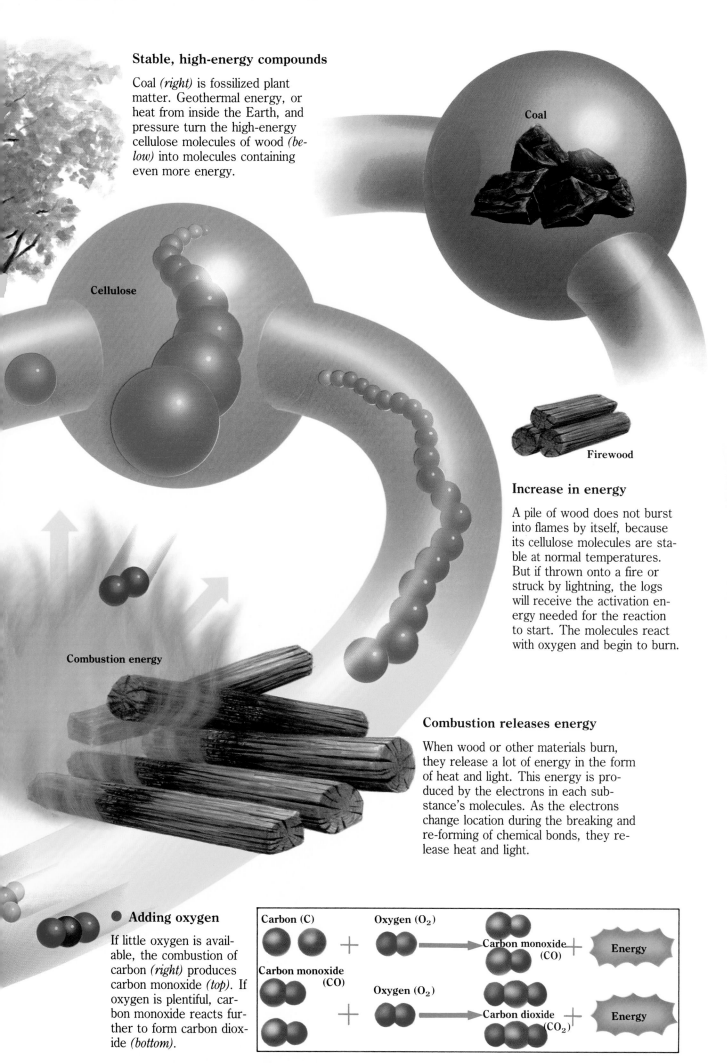

Stable, high-energy compounds

Coal *(right)* is fossilized plant matter. Geothermal energy, or heat from inside the Earth, and pressure turn the high-energy cellulose molecules of wood *(below)* into molecules containing even more energy.

Coal

Cellulose

Firewood

Increase in energy

A pile of wood does not burst into flames by itself, because its cellulose molecules are stable at normal temperatures. But if thrown onto a fire or struck by lightning, the logs will receive the activation energy needed for the reaction to start. The molecules react with oxygen and begin to burn.

Combustion energy

Combustion releases energy

When wood or other materials burn, they release a lot of energy in the form of heat and light. This energy is produced by the electrons in each substance's molecules. As the electrons change location during the breaking and re-forming of chemical bonds, they release heat and light.

● Adding oxygen

If little oxygen is available, the combustion of carbon *(right)* produces carbon monoxide *(top)*. If oxygen is plentiful, carbon monoxide reacts further to form carbon dioxide *(bottom)*.

Carbon (C)   Oxygen (O_2)   Carbon monoxide $+$ Energy
                                             (CO)

Carbon monoxide   Oxygen (O_2)   Carbon dioxide $+$ Energy
(CO)   (CO_2)

How Does Water Extinguish a Fire?

Three conditions are necessary to keep a fire burning: There must be oxygen, a material that burns, and enough heat to keep the combustion reaction going. If even one of these is missing, the fire stops burning. Water will extinguish most fires because it reduces the heat in the burning material. The first splash of water that touches a burning object turns to steam, which moves rapidly away from the fire and carries with it some of the energy produced by the combustion. As more water pours onto the fire, it continues to turn to steam and remove heat. Eventually the water robs the fire of enough heat and energy to lower its temperature below the point at which combustion reactions occur, and the fire goes out.

Many fire extinguishers contain carbon dioxide or a foam instead of water. These smother fires by preventing oxygen from reaching the burning material and also help in lowering the temperature.

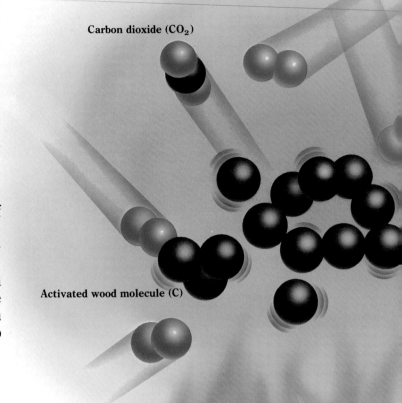

Carbon dioxide (CO_2)

Activated wood molecule (C)

Putting out a fire

Priming combustion

Wood consists of cellulose and other substances that will burn. But wood will burn only if it is heated enough to trigger combustion reactions between cellulose and oxygen, a process called activation.

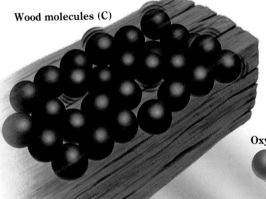

Wood molecules (C)

A fire begins

Once activation occurs and combustion begins, the temperature of the wood and the surrounding air rises rapidly. The increased heat speeds up the rate of combustion, and the fire grows in intensity.

Oxygen molecules (O_2)

Heat

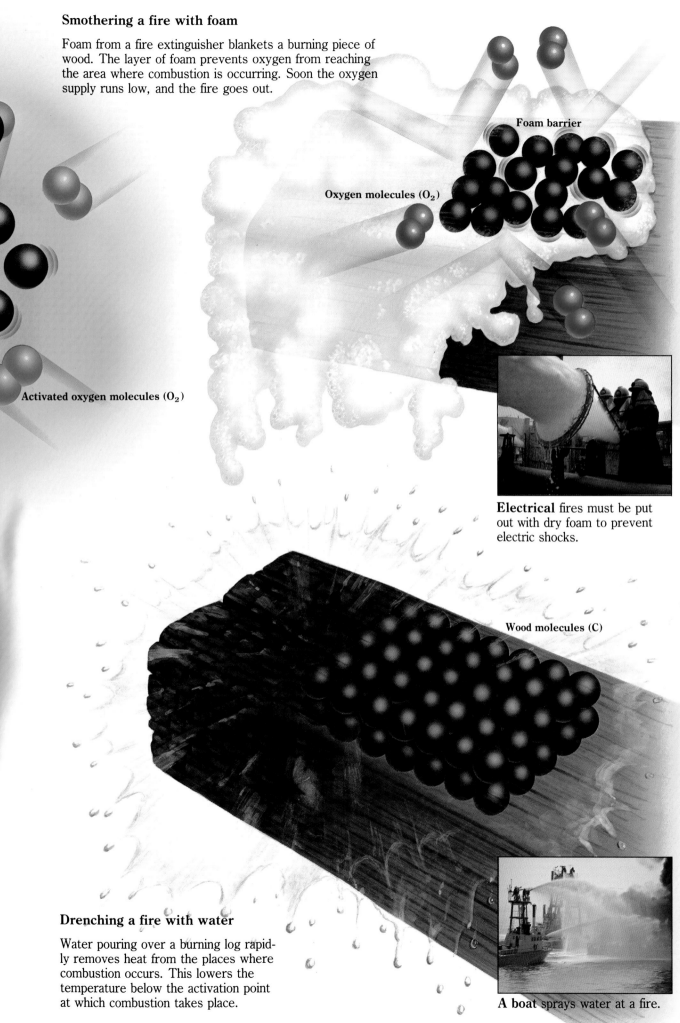

Smothering a fire with foam

Foam from a fire extinguisher blankets a burning piece of wood. The layer of foam prevents oxygen from reaching the area where combustion is occurring. Soon the oxygen supply runs low, and the fire goes out.

Foam barrier

Oxygen molecules (O_2)

Activated oxygen molecules (O_2)

Electrical fires must be put out with dry foam to prevent electric shocks.

Wood molecules (C)

Drenching a fire with water

Water pouring over a burning log rapidly removes heat from the places where combustion occurs. This lowers the temperature below the activation point at which combustion takes place.

A boat sprays water at a fire.

If Steel Wool Burns, Why Doesn't a Block of Steel?

Organic materials such as wood or coal are not the only things that burn. Metals, too, go through combustion in the presence of oxygen and heat. In many instances, however, metals only burn in a certain form. A block of iron or steel held over a flame does not burn, but a piece of steel wool ignites readily. Though the two are the same chemical material, the iron in steel wool is surrounded by far more oxygen and becomes hotter faster than a massive block of iron. The iron threads in steel wool allow a greater number of energetic iron atoms to come in contact with energetic oxygen, giving the material a better chance to burn than if the iron atoms were pressed together in a block of iron.

Other metals behave the same way. A magnesium block will burn only if heated for a long time, but a ribbon of magnesium burns in a violent flash, which makes it useful in disposable flash-bulbs. Similarly, aluminum foil is a good food wrap because it can withstand high temperatures, but aluminum powder ignites explosively and serves well as rocket fuel. Even substances that usually burn slowly will ignite with explosive force when they are in a form with a large surface area. Coal dust burns instantaneously. Grain dust is so explosive that one spark in a dust-filled grain elevator usually leads to disaster.

Activated iron atoms

Materials with a large surface area, such as steel wool *(below, left),* burn, unlike a solid block of iron *(below).* Because more material is exposed to oxygen in steel wool, more atoms can react.

Combustion of steel wool

The threadlike structure of steel wool allows many iron atoms to come in contact with oxygen atoms *(below).* The structure aids combustion by permitting oxygen to circulate among the iron threads.

Steel wool burns in the flame of an alcohol lamp.

Ribbons and blocks

Though a block of magnesium is not likely to burn, magnesium powder or ribbons, as in the flashbulb at right, burn at 650° C., or 1,200° F.

Magnesium block

Magnesium flashbulb

Aluminum powder and blocks

Powdered aluminum burns so rapidly that it seems to explode. A block of aluminum reacts only slowly with oxygen and will not burn easily.

Aluminum block

Aluminum powder powers the shuttle.

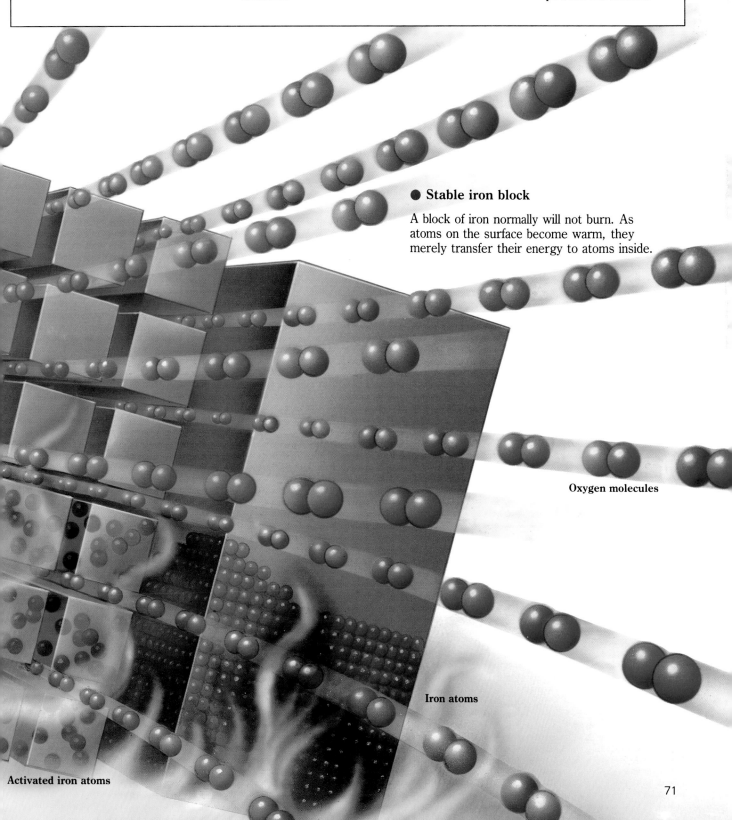

● Stable iron block

A block of iron normally will not burn. As atoms on the surface become warm, they merely transfer their energy to atoms inside.

Oxygen molecules

Iron atoms

Activated iron atoms

How Does an Ink Remover Work?

For as long as people have been writing with ink, they have been making mistakes that they wished they could erase. One type of ink remover scrubs the ink from the paper; another remover does not erase the mistake but renders it invisible by reacting with the substances that give ink its color. The blue-black ink used in most pens today contains two dyes. The black dye is the compound ferrous tannate, or metal gall. The tannin was originally derived from galls—the growths on plants formed by insects—and was combined with iron salts. Today the compound is produced in the laboratory. Ferrous tannate is colorless, but as soon as it hits the paper it reacts with oxygen in the air to become ferric tannate, which is bluish black and insoluble in water. Since it is hard to write with clear ink, modern pen ink also contains a blue dye that makes writing visible before the ferric tannate has time to form a more permanent mark.

Removing the two dyes in blue-black ink re-quires two separate chemical reactions. In the first reaction, oxalic acid, a bleaching agent, reacts with ferric tannate and reduces the oxygen in the mixture to restore it to the colorless ferrous tannate. The ink spot fades as this reaction takes place. In the second reaction, sodium hypochlorite, the whitening agent in laundry bleach, destroys the molecules that made the remaining dye blue, and the ink spot disappears.

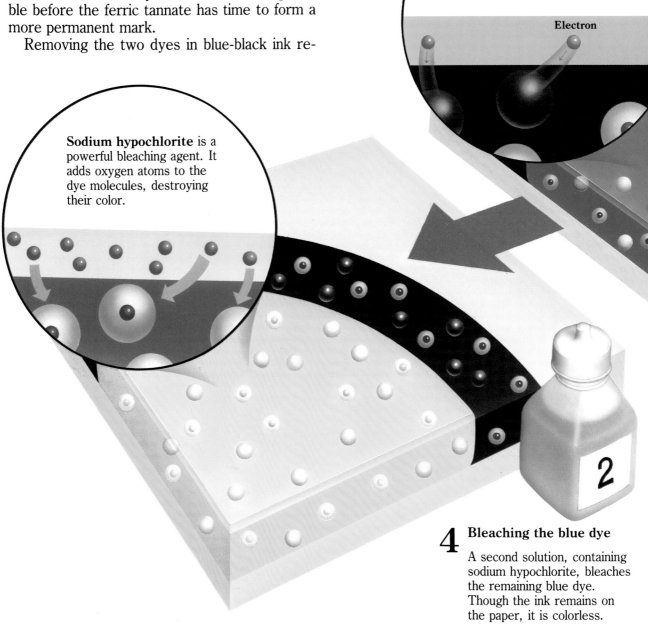

Oxalic acid gives an electron to ferric tannate, turning it into ferrous tannate, making the dye fade.

Electron

Sodium hypochlorite is a powerful bleaching agent. It adds oxygen atoms to the dye molecules, destroying their color.

4 Bleaching the blue dye

A second solution, containing sodium hypochlorite, bleaches the remaining blue dye. Though the ink remains on the paper, it is colorless.

- ⚪ Ferrous tannate
- ⚫ Ferric tannate
- ◉ Blue dye
- ◎ Bleached blue dye
- ● Oxygen atom
- ◖◗ Oxygen molecule

1 **The two dyes in ink**

Blue-black ink looks blue in its bottle because the black dye is still in its colorless state. The blue dye does not depend on reacting with oxygen for its color.

2 **Oxidizing ferrous tannate**

When the ink is applied to the paper, oxygen in the air begins reacting with the colorless ferrous tannate, converting it to black ferric tannate. Small black particles —each containing trillions of ferric tannate molecules—form as this reaction continues. The particles settle onto the paper, and a black ink mark appears.

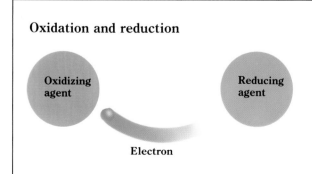

3 **Reducing ferric tannate**

Ink removal starts with a drop of water containing oxalic acid. The acid reduces ferric tannate back to the colorless ferrous tannate, and the black particles vanish.

Oxidation and reduction

Oxidizing agent

Reducing agent

Electron

In a redox reaction, or oxidation-reduction reaction, an oxidizing agent gains electrons from the oxidized compound and is reduced, while the reducing agent loses electrons to the reduced compound and is oxidized. The two processes are always connected, with oxidation taking place at the anode and reduction at the cathode.

Why Is Hydrogen Used as Rocket Fuel?

When the space shuttle roars into the sky, it is powered by the force of tiny molecules thrust out of the rocket's engines at a velocity of 3,536 meters per second, or 7,910 miles per hour. That enormous thrust is enough to lift the 2-million-kilogram, or 4.4-million-pound, spacecraft into orbit about 480 kilometers, or 290 miles, above the Earth's surface. The power comes from the combustion of hydrogen and oxygen inside the shuttle's three engines. A rocket's thrust comes from the speed and volume of the exhaust gases produced by its engines. The combustion reaction between hydrogen and oxygen occurs at extremely high temperatures. This propels the exhaust gas, which is mostly water vapor, out of the engine at great speed. Kerosene was used in older rockets, but the combustion product of kerosene is carbon dioxide, which is heavier than water. Because the momentum of the exhaust is figured by mass times velocity, kerosene's exhaust velocity is lower than hydrogen's.

● **Vintage A-2 rocket**

Heat of combustion

One gram, or 0.035 ounce, of hydrogen burned at 25° C., or 77° F., releases 4.6 times as much energy produced as heat by fuel combustion as 1 gram of aluminum.

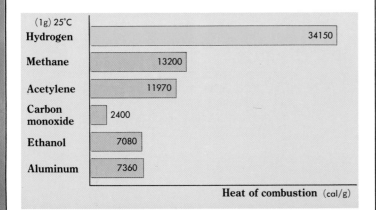

(1g) 25°C	Heat of combustion (cal/g)
Hydrogen	34150
Methane	13200
Acetylene	11970
Carbon monoxide	2400
Ethanol	7080
Aluminum	7360

● **Solid-fuel boosters**

Two solid-fuel rockets provide the thrust to lift the space shuttle by burning a mix of aluminum powder and an oxygen-rich chemical.

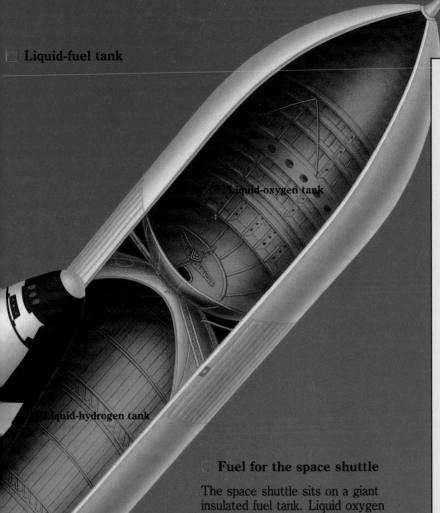

Liquid-fuel tank

Liquid-oxygen tank

Liquid-hydrogen tank

Fuel for the space shuttle

The space shuttle sits on a giant insulated fuel tank. Liquid oxygen fills the top compartment *(above)*, liquid hydrogen the bottom *(left)*.

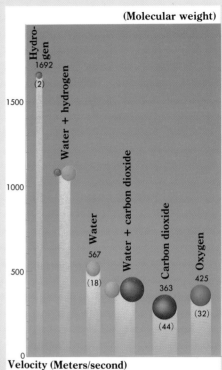

● Exhaust velocity

Exhaust velocity depends in part on the molecular weight of the gases. Hydrogen is the lightest and fastest, so any unburned hydrogen in the exhaust provides extra thrust.

(Molecular weight)

Hydrogen 1692 (2)

Water + hydrogen

Water 567 (18)

Water + carbon dioxide

Carbon dioxide 363 (44)

Oxygen 425 (32)

1500

1000

500

0

Velocity (Meters/second)

Combustion of hydrogen

Each shuttle engine burns hydrogen and oxygen in two stages. Hydrogen and a small amount of oxygen burn in two auxiliary combustion chambers. This drives high-pressure turbines that pump oxygen and hydrogen into the main combustion chamber. Some of the liquid hydrogen is used as a coolant to keep the engine from melting under the constant high temperatures of the combustion process. The liquid hydrogen vaporizes and becomes part of the exhaust.

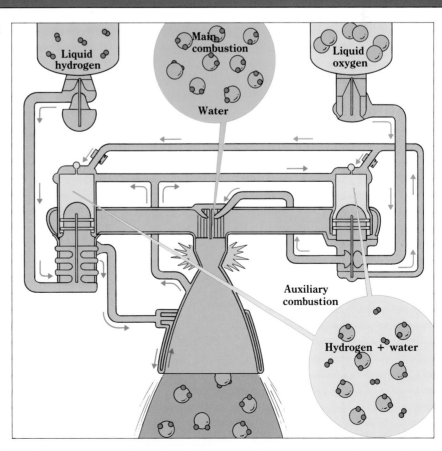

Liquid hydrogen

Main combustion

Liquid oxygen

Water

Auxiliary combustion

Hydrogen + water

What Causes the Ozone Hole?

High above the Earth in the stratosphere, a small number of ozone molecules shield all life from harmful ultraviolet radiation. Ozone, an unstable form of oxygen containing three oxygen atoms (O_3), falls apart into an oxygen atom (O) and an oxygen molecule (O_2) when it absorbs ultraviolet radiation. However, a fresh supply of ozone forms continually in the stratosphere, producing a delicate chemical balance in which a layer of less than 4.5 trillion kilograms (5 billion tons) of ozone, about three or four ozone molecules for every million molecules of air, blankets the Earth. That balance is threatened by chemicals called chlorofluorocarbons, or CFCs, such as the fluorocarbon 11 shown here. These substances —used in air conditioners, refrigerators, and industrial processes—rise to the stratosphere. There they decompose and release chlorine atoms, which cause ozone to break down. The difference is that each chlorine atom destroys as many as 100,000 ozone molecules, faster than nature can replenish them. As a result, the ozone layer is thinning, forming a hole that lets damaging ultraviolet radiation reach the Earth.

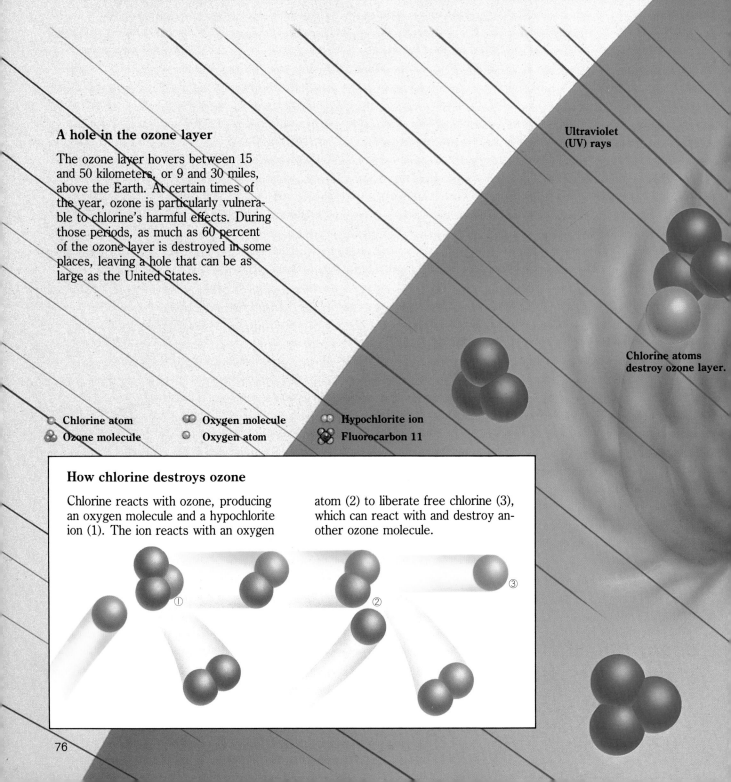

A hole in the ozone layer

The ozone layer hovers between 15 and 50 kilometers, or 9 and 30 miles, above the Earth. At certain times of the year, ozone is particularly vulnerable to chlorine's harmful effects. During those periods, as much as 60 percent of the ozone layer is destroyed in some places, leaving a hole that can be as large as the United States.

Ultraviolet (UV) rays

Chlorine atoms destroy ozone layer.

Chlorine atom   Oxygen molecule   Hypochlorite ion
Ozone molecule   Oxygen atom   Fluorocarbon 11

How chlorine destroys ozone

Chlorine reacts with ozone, producing an oxygen molecule and a hypochlorite ion (1). The ion reacts with an oxygen atom (2) to liberate free chlorine (3), which can react with and destroy another ozone molecule.

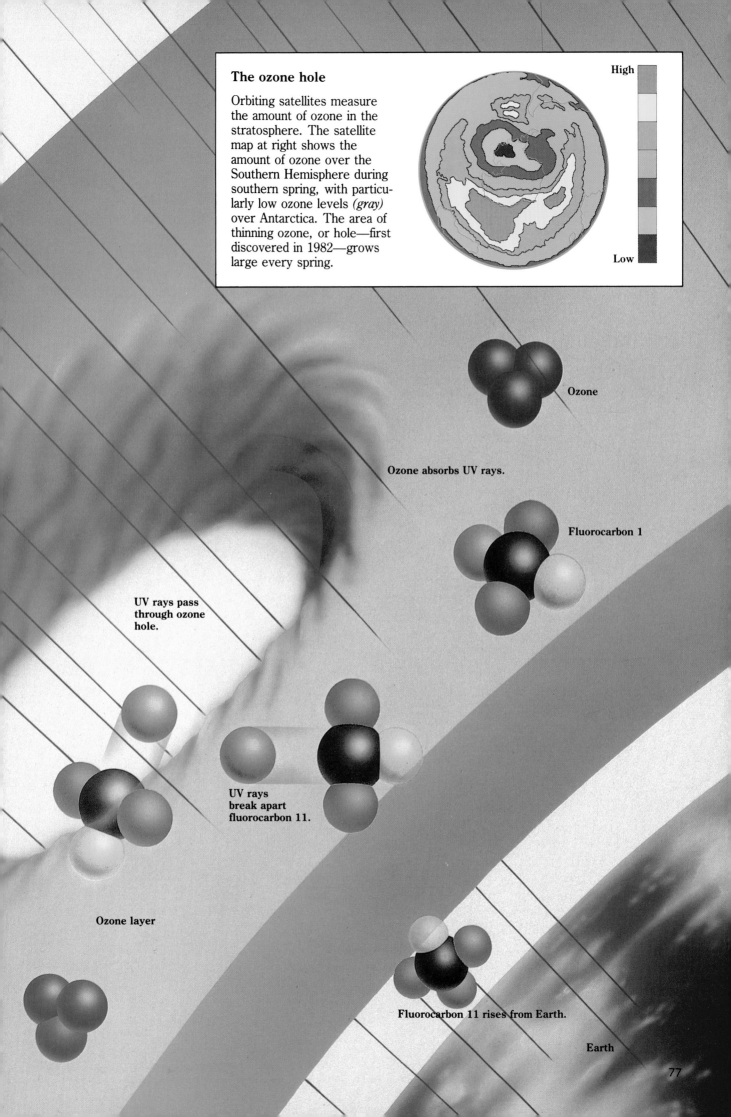

The ozone hole

Orbiting satellites measure the amount of ozone in the stratosphere. The satellite map at right shows the amount of ozone over the Southern Hemisphere during southern spring, with particularly low ozone levels *(gray)* over Antarctica. The area of thinning ozone, or hole—first discovered in 1982—grows large every spring.

High

Low

Ozone

Ozone absorbs UV rays.

Fluorocarbon 1

UV rays pass through ozone hole.

UV rays break apart fluorocarbon 11.

Ozone layer

Fluorocarbon 11 rises from Earth.

Earth

4
The Chemistry of Food

In few areas are chemical reactions more apparent than in the production and preparation of food. When a raw egg is boiled, for example, a chemical change transforms the egg's protein molecules from liquid to solid. In the treatment of other foods, atoms break apart or combine to form new compounds. Because some foods are difficult to enjoy in their natural state, cooks and scientists alike have found ways to make them tastier and safer to eat, and each new preparation involves changes in the foods' molecular structures. Flour becomes easier to digest when it has been cooked or baked, as in a loaf of bread. Adding certain bacteria to milk alters both its flavor and its texture. Various preservation techniques allow foods to be stored for long periods without spoilage. Each of these changes involves a rearrangement of atoms, resulting in a different consistency and flavor.

Such culinary strategies, developed through centuries of trial and error, are all part of the branch of chemistry known as food science. This chapter explores various foods and the chemical changes associated with their production and preparation.

The process by which an apple ripens and turns red involves chemical change, as do the reactions that cause it to turn brown when it is sliced open.

Why Does a Sliced Apple Turn Brown?

An apple that has been cut open turns brown because molecules called phenols that are in the skin and around the seeds protect the apple. When an apple is sliced or peeled, special enzymes take oxygen from the air and combine it with the phenols in the exposed flesh to produce polyphenols. The polyphenols react further with the enzymes and oxygen to create a form of the molecule quinone, which links with other molecules to produce a brown pigment that covers the apple's exposed flesh. This pigment forms a protective barrier that blocks the advance of harmful oxygen molecules through the apple's interior.

To prevent a cut apple from turning brown, it must be kept from oxygen in the air. Dipping slices in water is the simplest solution. Coating the exposed surfaces with vitamin C works even better. Since the vitamin reacts faster with oxygen than the phenols do, the brown pigment does not form and the apple stays white.

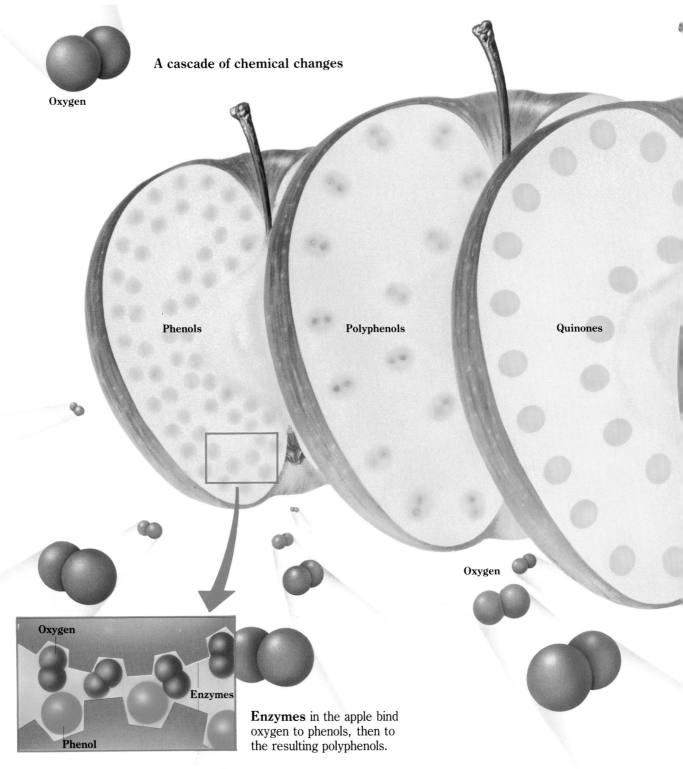

A cascade of chemical changes

Oxygen

Phenols

Polyphenols

Quinones

Oxygen

Oxygen

Phenol

Enzymes

Enzymes in the apple bind oxygen to phenols, then to the resulting polyphenols.

Ways to prevent browning

Placing apple slices in water protects the open surfaces from the oxygen that starts the browning process. Coating the surfaces with vitamin C, found in products such as lemon juice, or adding vitamin C to the water will keep the apples white.

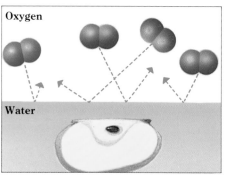

Water shields the apple from oxygen.

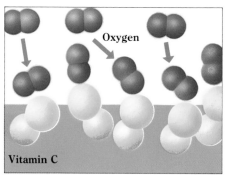

Oxygen binds to vitamin C.

Building a chemical wall

The brown pigment that forms on the apple is like a wall created by the oxidation of the exposed outer cells. This wall slows down the rate at which oxygen reaches the interior flesh of the apple. Many other fruits and vegetables, including bananas and potatoes, turn brown for the same reason.

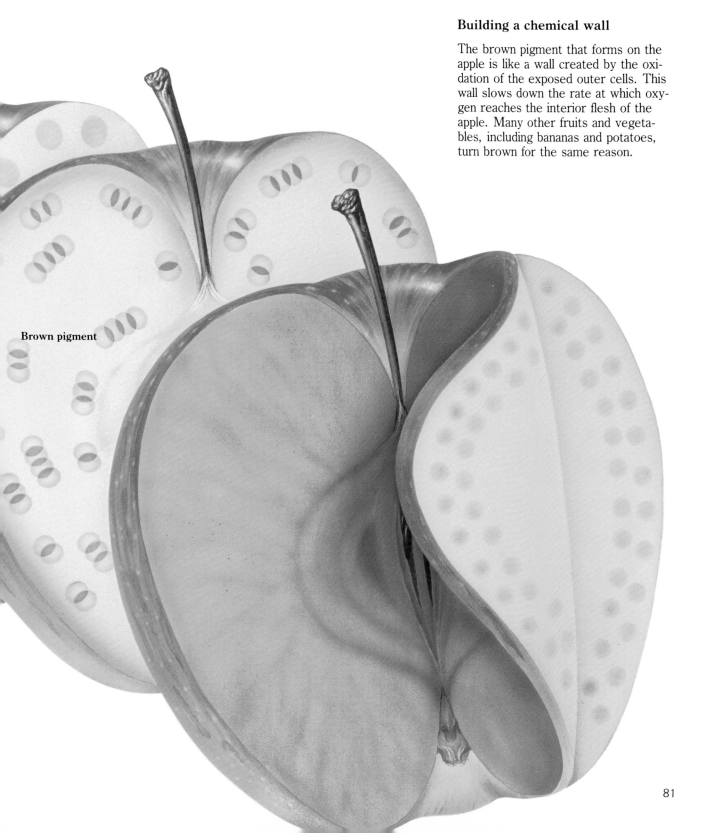

Brown pigment

Are All Sour Foods Acidic?

Not all sour foods can be classified as acidic, even though they may appear to be so at first. The lemon, for example, tastes sour and tests highly acidic, but it is classified as a basic, or alkaline, food. The lemon's high content of sodium, potassium, calcium, and magnesium—substances that, when mixed with water, show up as alkaline in laboratory tests—is the cause for this rating. Conversely, foods that contain substances such as chlorine, phosphorus, or sulfur, all of which show acidity when they are mixed with water, are categorized as acidic. Such foods include carrots and spinach.

To determine if a food is acidic or alkaline, scientists first heat it until all that remains are ashes—a process that mimics the digestive process that occurs in humans. They then dissolve the ashes in water and measure the acidity of the solution, determining its pH value.

Converting food by combustion

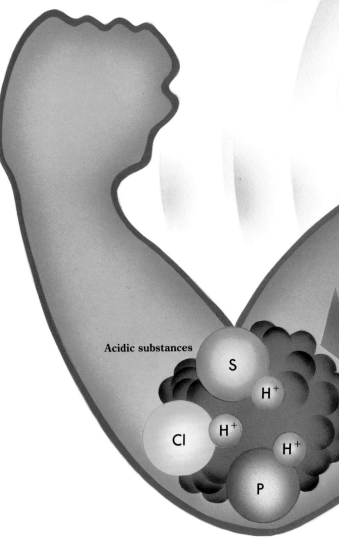

Acidic substances

S Sulfur	**Cl** Chlorine	**Ca** Calcium	**OH⁻** Hydroxide ions
P Phosphorus	**Mg** Magnesium	**K** Potassium	**H⁺** Hydrogen ions

Simulating digestion

By heating a food until only ashes remain, chemists can determine if the food is acidic or alkaline. The ashes, which simulate in part the waste products of human digestion, are dissolved in water and then tested for acidity.

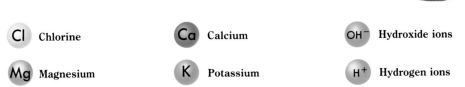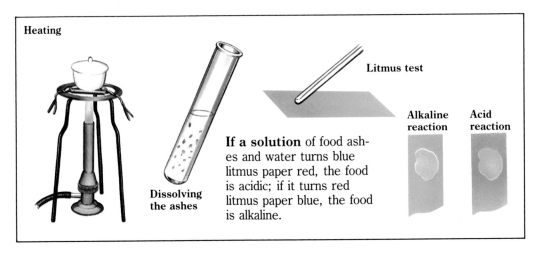

Heating

Litmus test

Dissolving the ashes

If a solution of food ashes and water turns blue litmus paper red, the food is acidic; if it turns red litmus paper blue, the food is alkaline.

Alkaline reaction   Acid reaction

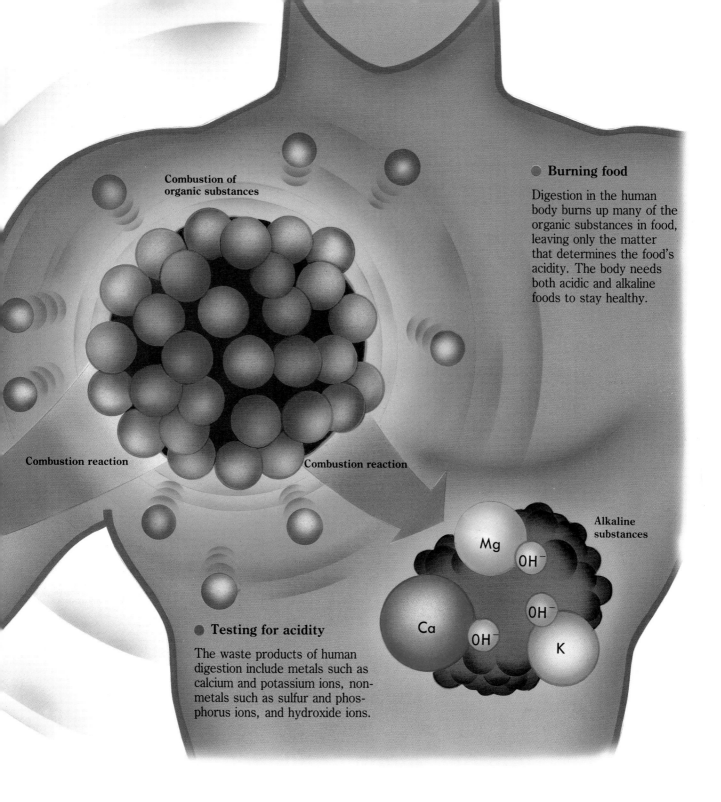

Combustion of organic substances

● Burning food

Digestion in the human body burns up many of the organic substances in food, leaving only the matter that determines the food's acidity. The body needs both acidic and alkaline foods to stay healthy.

Combustion reaction

Combustion reaction

Alkaline substances

Mg

OH⁻

OH⁻

Ca

OH⁻

K

● Testing for acidity

The waste products of human digestion include metals such as calcium and potassium ions, non-metals such as sulfur and phosphorus ions, and hydroxide ions.

The pH scale

The ribbon below indicates the acidity or alkalinity of substances on the pH scale, which ranges from 0 to 14, with 7 being neutral. Foods with a low pH value are acidic, while those with high values are alkaline. The pH of human blood is 7.4, which is nearly neutral. Milk measures an acid 6.5, oranges 3.5. Ammonia registers an alkaline value of 12.

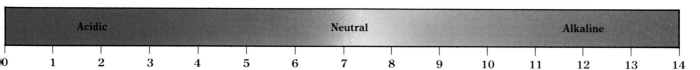

Acidic						Neutral					Alkaline		
0	1	2	3	4	5	6	7	8	9	10	11	12	13	14

How Is Yogurt Made?

In the days before refrigeration and modern processing of milk, early nomadic herdsmen searched for a way to preserve milk and transport it without spilling. Their solution was to ferment milk, a process that turns it into semisolid yogurt. Today yogurt is still valued because it is easy to digest and refreshing as a snack.

The yogurtmaking process begins when raw milk is pasteurized, or heated to 82° C., or 180° F., to kill any bacteria that may live in it. A yogurt culture is added to the pasteurized milk, and the mixture is incubated at temperatures between 37° and 45° C., or 100° and 113° F., which converts the milk's natural sugars to acids, or ferments it. The newly formed acids connect the milk's protein chains into large, complex networks, turning liquid milk into tart yogurt.

Other foods produced from fermented milk include sour cream, cheese, and buttermilk.

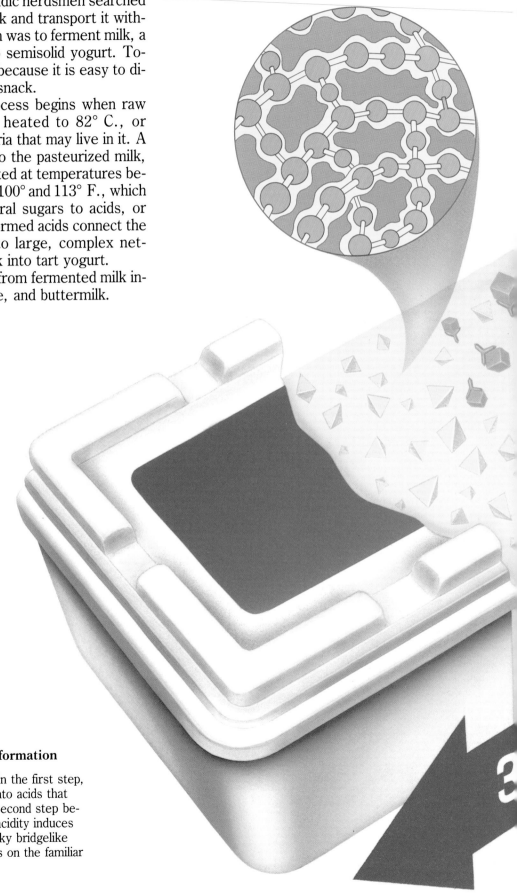

Semisolid milk

The acids unleashed by fermentation cause the individual protein chains in milk to link together *(above, right)*. As a result of this linkage, the milk becomes less fluid and gradually begins to congeal.

The two stages of yogurt formation

Yogurt forms in two stages. In the first step, bacteria break sugars down into acids that raise the milk's acidity. The second step begins as the milk's increasing acidity induces protein molecules to form bulky bridgelike structures, and the milk takes on the familiar semisolid form of yogurt.

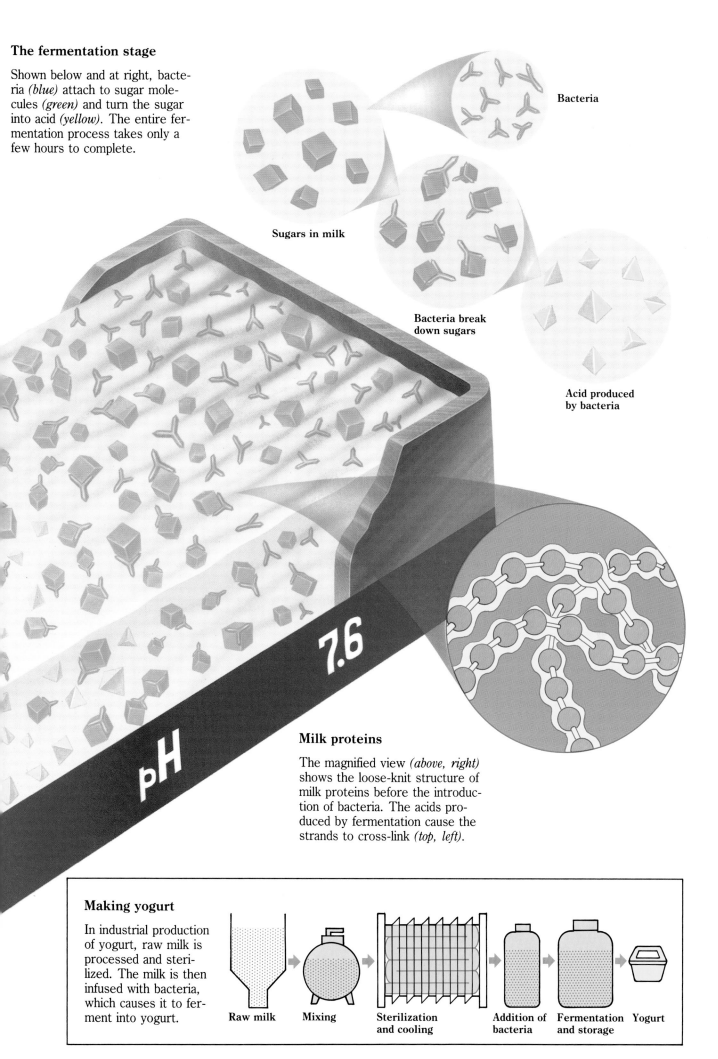

The fermentation stage

Shown below and at right, bacteria *(blue)* attach to sugar molecules *(green)* and turn the sugar into acid *(yellow)*. The entire fermentation process takes only a few hours to complete.

Bacteria

Sugars in milk

Bacteria break down sugars

Acid produced by bacteria

pH

7.6

Milk proteins

The magnified view *(above, right)* shows the loose-knit structure of milk proteins before the introduction of bacteria. The acids produced by fermentation cause the strands to cross-link *(top, left)*.

Making yogurt

In industrial production of yogurt, raw milk is processed and sterilized. The milk is then infused with bacteria, which causes it to ferment into yogurt.

Raw milk   Mixing   Sterilization and cooling   Addition of bacteria   Fermentation and storage   Yogurt

Why Does Instant Coffee Dissolve?

There are two ways to make instant coffee: the freeze-dry method and the spray-dry method. Both start identically as coffee beans are roasted, ground, and brewed with boiling water to produce a concentrated liquid. In the freeze-dry method, the liquid is frozen at a temperature of $-40°$ C., or $-40°$ F. The frozen coffee is then crumbled into small granules and placed in a vacuum drying machine. In a vacuum the ice in the coffee granules sublimes, or changes directly from solid to gas, leaving behind porous crystals of instant coffee.

The spray-dry method involves spraying concentrated coffee through a stream of hot air. The coffee's water instantly evaporates, yielding a fine powder that is then processed into crystals similar to those formed by freeze-drying.

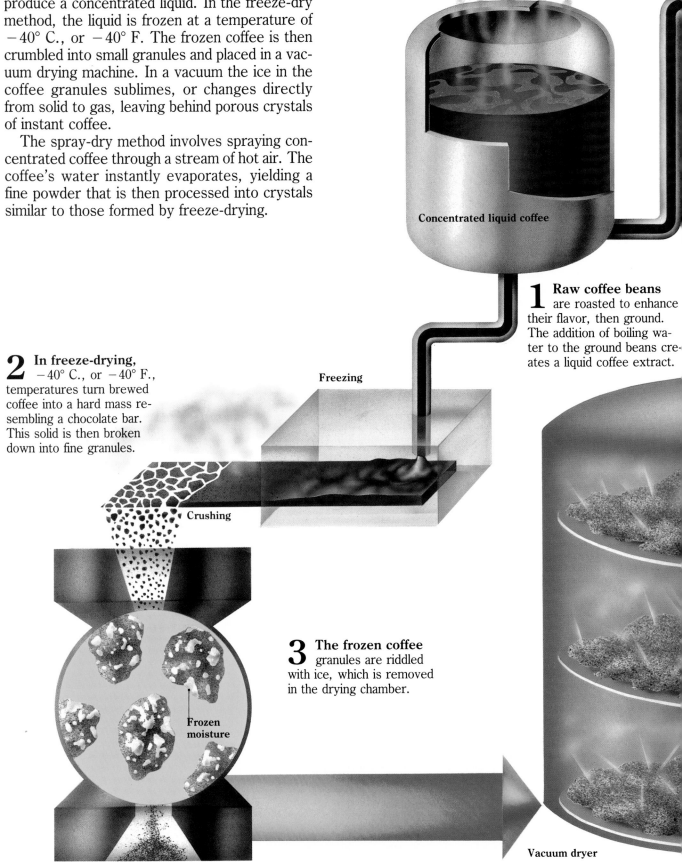

Two routes to instant coffee

Concentrated liquid coffee

1 **Raw coffee beans** are roasted to enhance their flavor, then ground. The addition of boiling water to the ground beans creates a liquid coffee extract.

2 **In freeze-drying,** $-40°$ C., or $-40°$ F., temperatures turn brewed coffee into a hard mass resembling a chocolate bar. This solid is then broken down into fine granules.

Freezing

Crushing

3 **The frozen coffee** granules are riddled with ice, which is removed in the drying chamber.

Frozen moisture

Vacuum dryer

2 **Hot air** rushes through a mist of liquid coffee extract *(below),* evaporating the extract's water.

3 **The evaporating** water leaves behind particles of pure coffee, which combine into larger granules.

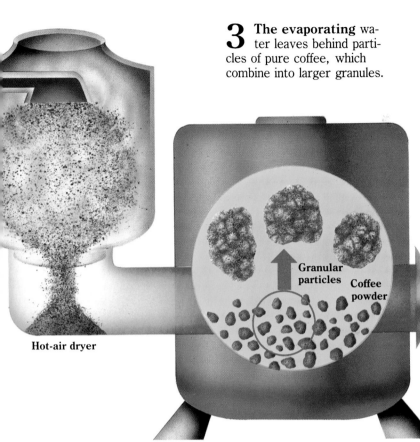

Granular particles   Coffee powder

Hot-air dryer

Powdered instant coffee is produced by the spray-dry method.

4 **The reduced** pressure in the drying chamber causes the ice in the coffee particles to sublime. What remains are porous granules of instant coffee.

Porous particles

Moisture evaporates

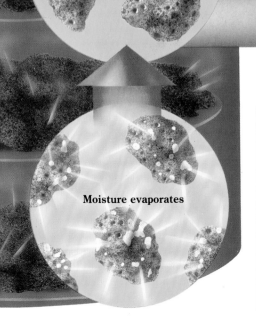

Granulated instant coffee is produced by freeze-drying.

Fast dissolution

Instant coffee dissolves quickly because its crystals are shot through with small holes. When water comes in contact with the crystals, it quickly seeps into these holes, dissolving the crystal from the inside as well as the outside.

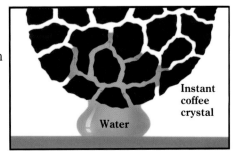

Instant coffee crystal

Water

How Are Foods Preserved?

Food spoils for two main reasons. In fruits and vegetables, the natural ripening process—caused by continued cellular respiration after the food is picked—can proceed too far, producing overripe, inedible food. Or, in a process that affects all foods, microorganisms that include bacteria, molds, and yeasts can attack the food and cause it to rot. Over the millennia scientists and cooks have developed a number of preserving methods that successfully delay or prevent these two processes.

Because food-spoiling microorganisms thrive only under specific conditions that include oxygen, moisture, and warm temperatures, it is possible to destroy the organisms by altering these conditions. Storing food at low temperatures or sterilizing it with heat delays spoilage. Other methods of preservation—either by vacuum-packing the food or storing it with some carbon dioxide—minimize exposure to oxygen, which causes overripening and fosters bacterial growth. Still other techniques include drying food and preserving it with salt or sugar.

The right conditions

Controlling spoilage is often a matter of making food less hospitable to harmful microorganisms. Decreasing the amount of moisture in the food, lowering the food's temperature, and increasing its acidity are all steps that accomplish this.

Methods of food preservation

The overripening process

Carbon dioxide

Controlled-atmosphere storage

Foods stored in controlled atmospheres of 1-3 percent carbon dioxide will slow their respiration and spoilage by reducing oxygen levels.

Suppressing respiration to slow down overripening

Taking in oxygen

Keeping it cool

Cold storage reduces a food's respiration and slows overripening. The low temperatures also limit the growth of harmful bacteria.

Vacuum-packed foods

Sealing food off from air—a process known as vacuum-packing—isolates the food from both oxygen and microorganisms. Foods that are preserved by this method keep their taste and aroma for a long time.

Canning

Canned food is sterilized by heat and then vacuum-packed to avoid contamination. Because food is relatively easy to can and, once in jars or cans, simple to transport and use, this is a popular method of preserving.

Preventing growth of microorganisms

Salt

Salt absorbs the water in food cells, depriving bacteria of the moisture they need to survive.

Using salt to preserve foods

Salt and sugar are used to draw moisture from foods. The lower a food's water content, the harder it is for bacteria to survive in it.

How fruits overripen

Fruits and vegetables ripen as their cells breathe, a process that requires oxygen. Overripening occurs when foods continue to take in oxygen even after they are ripe.

Oxygen changes foods

As food respires, it takes in oxygen and gives off carbon dioxide. At low oxygen levels, respiration decreases and slows down the ripening process.

Giving off carbon dioxide

Freezing

Freezing

Freezing puts foods in a kind of suspended animation. Cellular respiration and overripening stop, and the cold arrests the growth of bacteria.

What Goes into Food Flavor Enhancers?

Flavor enhancers are substances that increase a person's perception of different tastes. The most widely used food enhancer is monosodium glutamate, called MSG for short. MSG is derived from glutamic acid, one of the 20 amino acids the body uses to make proteins.

The industrial process for manufacturing MSG begins with molasses, a by-product of the refining of sugarcane. Fermented in a tank containing special bacteria, the molasses produces glutamic acid.

At this point, the glutamic acid molecules exist as two types. Although the individual atoms are connected in the same order, the two kinds of molecules are mirror images of each other. Only one type of molecule, called L-glutamic acid, acts as a flavor enhancer; the other one is inactive. Once isolated from its useless counterpart, the L-glutamic acid is turned into MSG by converting the acid into its sodium salt. After the MSG is decolored—so it will not alter the food's appearance—it is ready for use in cooking.

Not for everybody

While harmless to most people, monosodium glutamate, derived from sugarcane, may cause some people to experience headaches, stomachaches, drowsiness, and even stiffening of the joints.

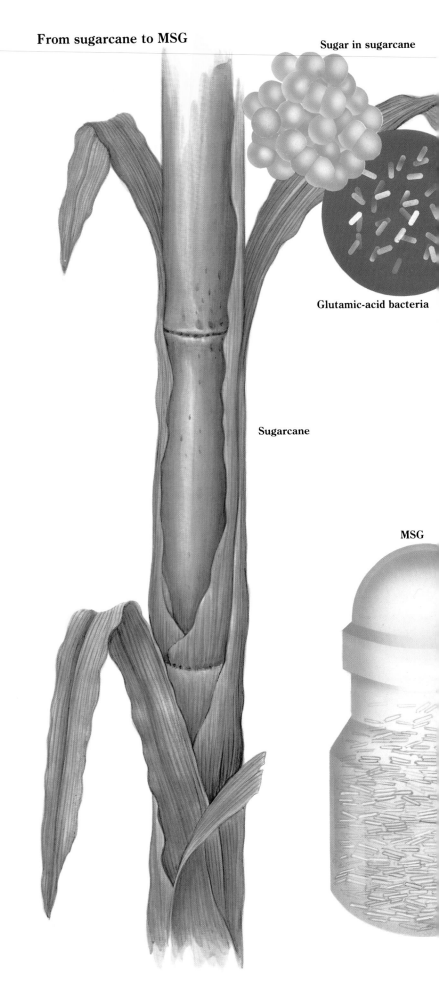

From sugarcane to MSG

Sugar in sugarcane

Glutamic-acid bacteria

Sugarcane

MSG

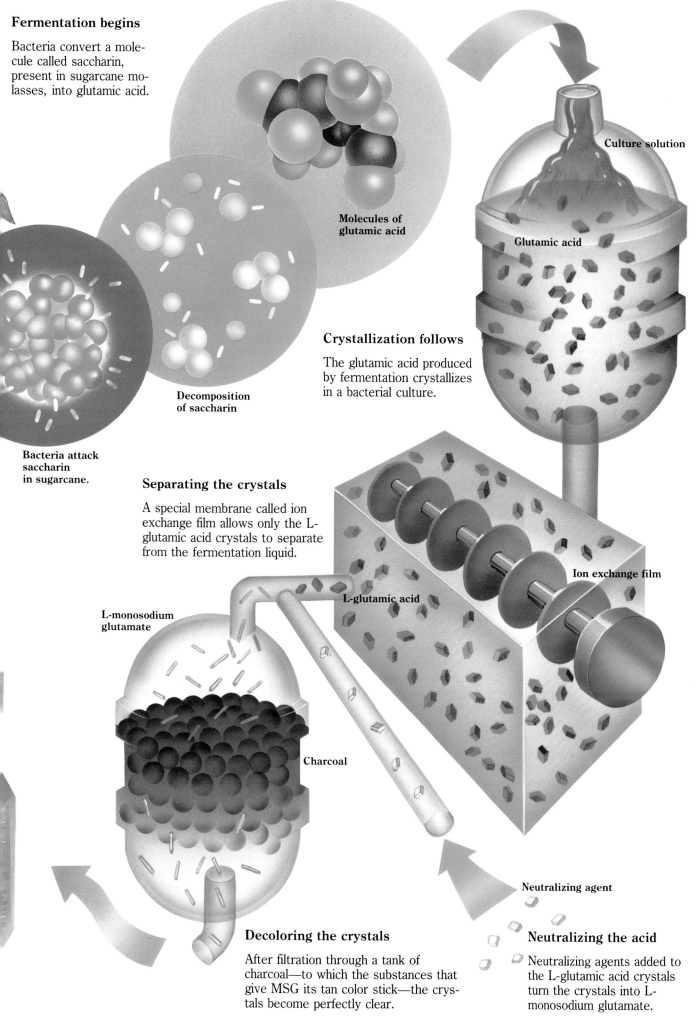

Fermentation begins

Bacteria convert a molecule called saccharin, present in sugarcane molasses, into glutamic acid.

Molecules of glutamic acid

Decomposition of saccharin

Bacteria attack saccharin in sugarcane.

Culture solution

Glutamic acid

Crystallization follows

The glutamic acid produced by fermentation crystallizes in a bacterial culture.

Separating the crystals

A special membrane called ion exchange film allows only the L-glutamic acid crystals to separate from the fermentation liquid.

L-glutamic acid

Ion exchange film

L-monosodium glutamate

Charcoal

Neutralizing agent

Decoloring the crystals

After filtration through a tank of charcoal—to which the substances that give MSG its tan color stick—the crystals become perfectly clear.

Neutralizing the acid

Neutralizing agents added to the L-glutamic acid crystals turn the crystals into L-monosodium glutamate.

91

Why Is Ice Cream Softer Than Ice?

Although ice cream contains a lot of water, it retains a fairly soft consistency at 0° C., or 32° F.—the temperature at which water freezes. The secret to ice cream's smooth consistency lies in the nature of its ingredients and the way they are combined.

To make ice cream, the ingredients—which include milk, cream, eggs, and other substances—are stirred together with sugar in a special freezer. At first only the water in the ingredients freezes, leaving particles of fat in liquid form. But as the stirring continues and the temperature decreases, tiny air bubbles become trapped in the mixture. These air bubbles, as well as the globules of fat, help separate the ice crystals, preventing the ice from forming large chunks that would turn the ice cream solid.

Some people like to make their own ice cream, using special home freezers. The ingredients are placed in a freezing chamber that is surrounded by salt and cracked ice to produce the necessary low temperatures. Then the mix is stirred by a special "dasher" that is driven by a hand crank or by an electric motor. Since a small machine cannot stir the ingredients as thoroughly as industrial ice cream makers, the homemade product usually contains less air and is not as smooth as commercial brands.

The structure of ice cream

Churning ice cream

The air whipped into ice cream during stirring is called overrun. If 1 pint of air is mixed into 1 pint of the ingredients, for example, the result is 2 pints of ice cream with an overrun of 100 percent. Ordinary ice cream usually has an overrun of 60-70 percent—meaning that air has increased the volume of the ice cream by that percentage—while the overrun in soft ice cream is 30-80 percent and 20-60 percent in sherbet.

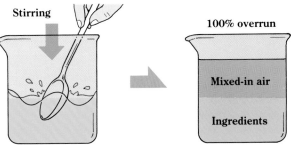

Stirring

100% overrun

Mixed-in air

Ingredients

A tasty mixture of solid, liquid, and gas

The two essential things for making ice cream are fat, supplied by the ingredients, and air bubbles, introduced by vigorous stirring.

Ice crystals

Fat globules

Air bubbles

1 **The tiny** air bubbles in ice cream are surrounded by ice crystals and small, liquid fat globules.

2 **As the** temperature drops, ice crystals tend to grow larger. But constant stirring prevents further growth, keeping the crystals small and apart from each other.

3 **At very cold** temperatures, the ice crystals become more numerous and the fat globules more concentrated. But air bubbles keep the ingredients from getting too hard.

Why foods have different freezing points

The freezing rates of various foods differ depending on their moisture contents. At −15° C., or 5° F., 93 percent of the milk and 88 percent of the onion—two foods with a high water content—will freeze. At the same temperature, only about 70 percent of the apple and the orange and 65 percent of the banana become frozen.

Milk 93%

Onion 88%

Apple 78%

Orange 73%

Banana 65%

Why Do Boiled Eggs Become Hard?

Protein molecules

Hardening of the protein

1 **The raw egg's protein** molecules are intertwined in complex three-dimensional structures. Because the individual proteins are able to move freely, both the egg white and the yolk remain liquid.

Egg yolk

Raw state at 65° C., or 149° F.

Soft boiled at 65°-85° C., or 149°-185° F.

Hard boiled at 85° C., or 185° F.

The liquid interior of a raw egg hardens when boiled in water because the water's intense heat changes the structure of the egg's proteins. At room temperature, the protein strands are tightly folded in a complex three-dimensional configuration. But at higher temperatures the strands loosen up, and as they unravel, their ends become exposed. These ends bond with other protein strands, fastening the individual proteins into a mesh that turns the egg solid.

Because the protein structures of egg yolk and egg white vary slightly, they harden at different temperatures. Up to 60° C., or 140° F., there is little change in either yolk or white. But above that temperature, the white part of the egg begins to resemble a semitransparent jelly. The yolk gets somewhat sticky at 65° C., or 149° F., and starts to harden at 70° C., or 158° F. At this temperature, the egg becomes soft boiled. The white hardens fully at 80° C., or 176° F., and at 85° C., or 185° F., both yolk and white are hard boiled.

2 **When the egg** is placed in boiling water, the convolutions in each protein strand begin to soften and straighten out. The protein ends, normally protected within the folds, become exposed.

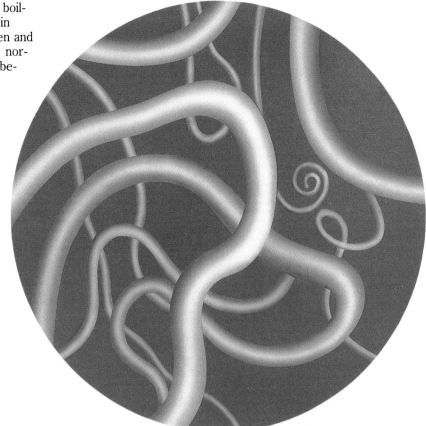

Egg white

Raw state up to 60° C., or 140° F.

60

Jelly forms at 60°-80° C., or 140°-176° F.

70

80

Hard boiled at 80° C., or 176° F.

90

(°C)

3 **When the temperature** reaches 60° C., or 140° F., the protein ends join together in bridgelike bonds; links also form at other points along the protein strands. These new bonds prevent the proteins from moving around freely, solidifying the egg.

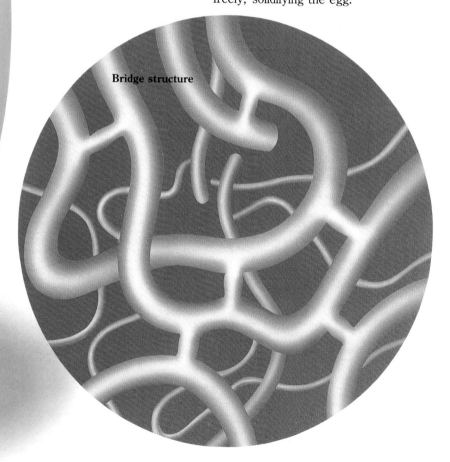

Bridge structure

How Is Salt Reclaimed from the Sea?

In the United States table salt is made by isolating it from underground brine deposits. But in countries with few salt deposits, salt is recovered from seawater. Because the sodium and chloride ions of table salt are electrically charged, they can be isolated by an electric current.

After being filtered to remove impurities, seawater is pumped into a tank with positive and negative electrodes at its ends. When a current passes through the electrodes, the ions begin to move: the positively charged sodium ions toward the negative electrode and the negatively charged chloride ions to the positive electrode.

As the ions move toward their respective poles, they must pass through membranes called ion exchange films. The first film, called negative ion exchange film, lets only negative ions through, while the other one, the positive ion exchange film, permits only positive ions to pass. An alternating arrangement of these films forces the sodium and chloride ions to accumulate, producing regions of concentrated salt water. The salt-rich water is then pumped out of the tank and evaporated, leaving only crystals of table salt.

The ion exchange method

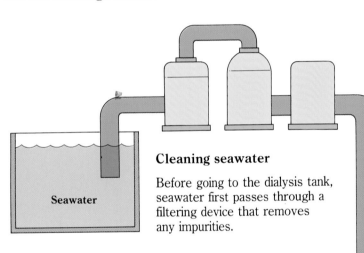

Cleaning seawater

Before going to the dialysis tank, seawater first passes through a filtering device that removes any impurities.

Seawater

Separating ions by charge

The positive ion exchange film allows positively charged sodium ions to pass while screening out negatively charged chloride ions. The negative ion exchange film does just the opposite.

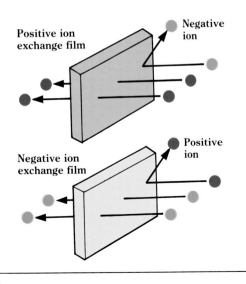

Positive ion exchange film

Negative ion

Negative ion exchange film

Positive ion

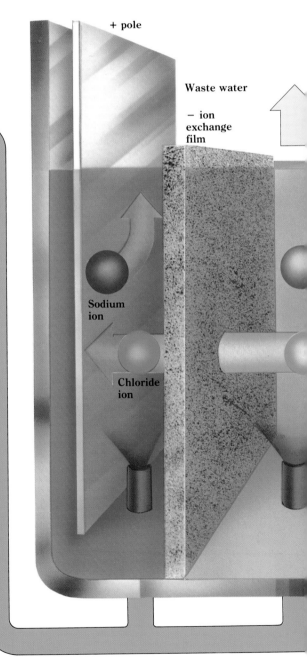

+ pole

Waste water

− ion exchange film

Sodium ion

Chloride ion

The dialysis tank greatly increases the salt concentration of seawater, which normally contains only about 3 percent salt.

Salt of the Earth

Various types of salt formations exist in nature. The Atacama Desert *(right)* in Chile is one example, as is the salt pond *(far right)* in an oasis in Niger. The salt pillars *(inset)* are formed from the pond's ruddy, mineral-laden water.

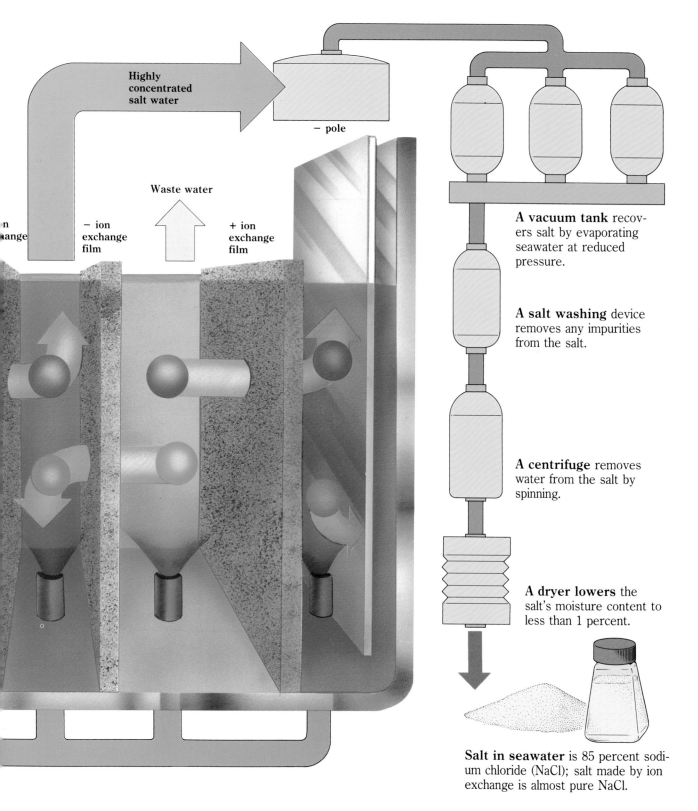

Highly concentrated salt water

− pole

Waste water

n
ange

− ion exchange film

+ ion exchange film

A vacuum tank recovers salt by evaporating seawater at reduced pressure.

A salt washing device removes any impurities from the salt.

A centrifuge removes water from the salt by spinning.

A dryer lowers the salt's moisture content to less than 1 percent.

Salt in seawater is 85 percent sodium chloride (NaCl); salt made by ion exchange is almost pure NaCl.

How Is Drinking Water Purified?

The purification of drinking water proceeds in several stages. The first step is sedimentation, in which large particles suspended in the water settle to the bottom. The second is filtration, in which suspended solids and harmful bacteria are strained out. In the third stage, chlorine, a powerful disinfectant, is added to the water to kill the remaining microorganisms.

Unfortunately, chlorine can give water a bad taste and in large doses can even cause serious health problems. A substitute used in some countries is ozone, a safe, tasteless gas consisting of three oxygen atoms bound together. But because ozone's germ-killing power does not last long, a tiny amount of chlorine must still be added for long-term disinfection.

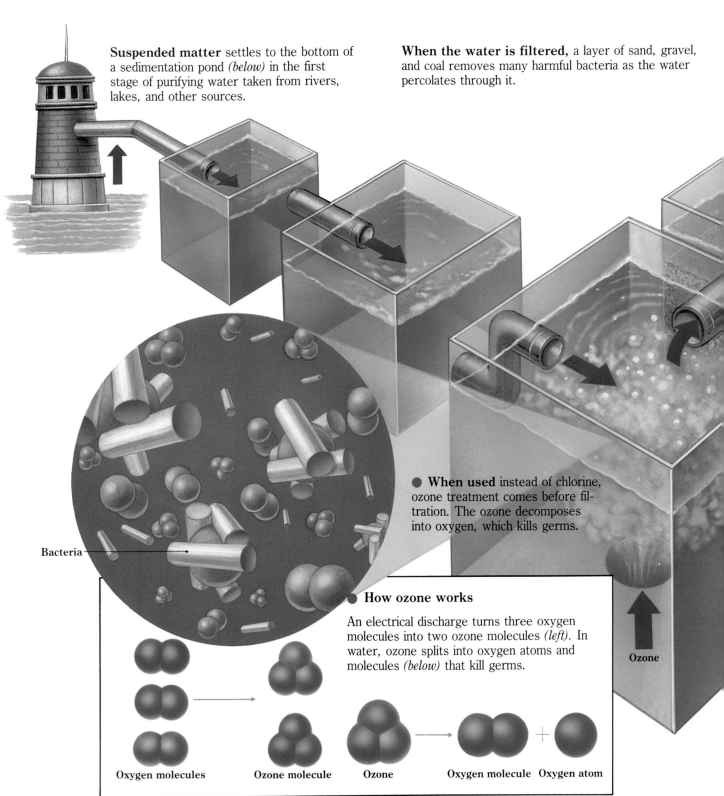

Suspended matter settles to the bottom of a sedimentation pond *(below)* in the first stage of purifying water taken from rivers, lakes, and other sources.

When the water is filtered, a layer of sand, gravel, and coal removes many harmful bacteria as the water percolates through it.

Bacteria

● **When used** instead of chlorine, ozone treatment comes before filtration. The ozone decomposes into oxygen, which kills germs.

● **How ozone works**

An electrical discharge turns three oxygen molecules into two ozone molecules *(left)*. In water, ozone splits into oxygen atoms and molecules *(below)* that kill germs.

Ozone

Oxygen molecules   Ozone molecule   Ozone   Oxygen molecule Oxygen atom

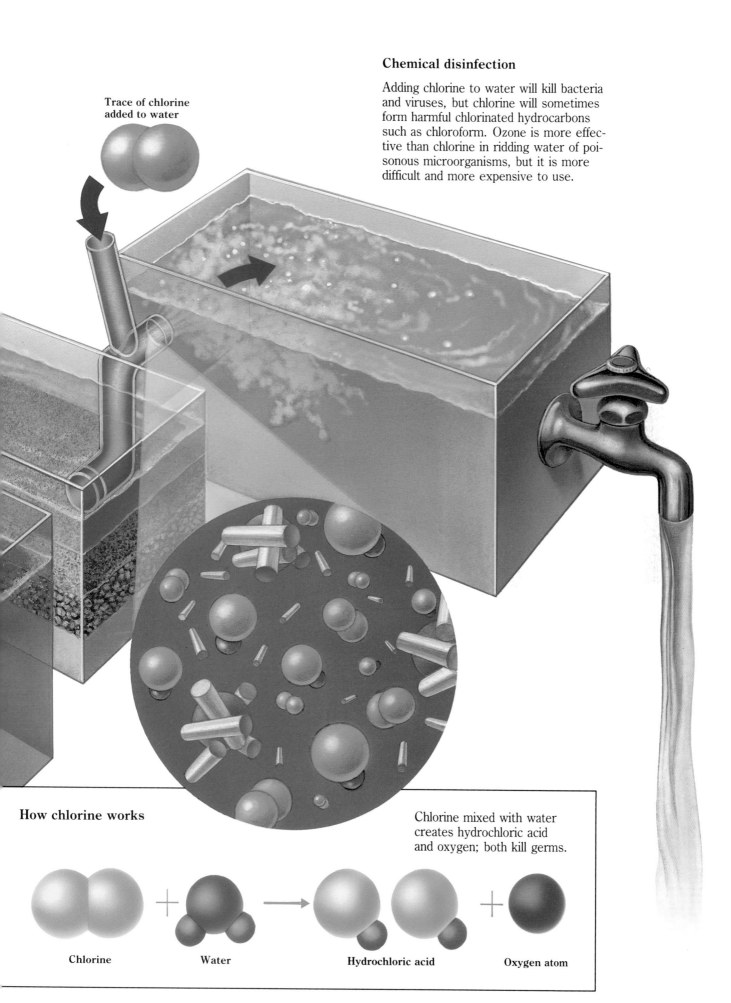

Trace of chlorine added to water

Chemical disinfection

Adding chlorine to water will kill bacteria and viruses, but chlorine will sometimes form harmful chlorinated hydrocarbons such as chloroform. Ozone is more effective than chlorine in ridding water of poisonous microorganisms, but it is more difficult and more expensive to use.

How chlorine works

Chlorine mixed with water creates hydrochloric acid and oxygen; both kill germs.

Chlorine   Water   Hydrochloric acid   Oxygen atom

Why Is Flour Cooked?

A major component of flour is starch, which consists of long chains of glucose molecules bound together. When raw, these chains form a rigid pattern, known as beta-starch, that resists digestion by the body's enzymes. But when the starch is boiled with water, or baked as in the loaf of bread at right, its crystalline structures begin to break down. Water molecules seep in between the glucose molecules, giving the starch a pastelike consistency called alpha-starch. Since enzymes can break down the alpha-starch, the flour is much easier to digest.

Unfortunately, alpha-starch returns to the beta-starch stage when the temperature falls and the moisture evaporates. This tendency, known as the aging phenomenon of starch, produces a hard form of beta-starch as in stale bread that is once again difficult to digest.

■ **Changing starch's structure**

The structure of starch

The raw starch, or beta-starch, contained in a kernel of wheat *(above)* consists of large, branched glucose chains with a regular, crystalline pattern.

Two views of starch

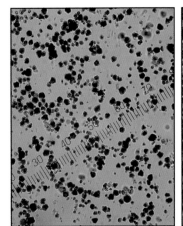 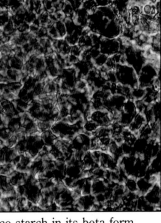

The photograph at left shows rice starch in its beta form, while the one at right shows the waterlogged alpha form.

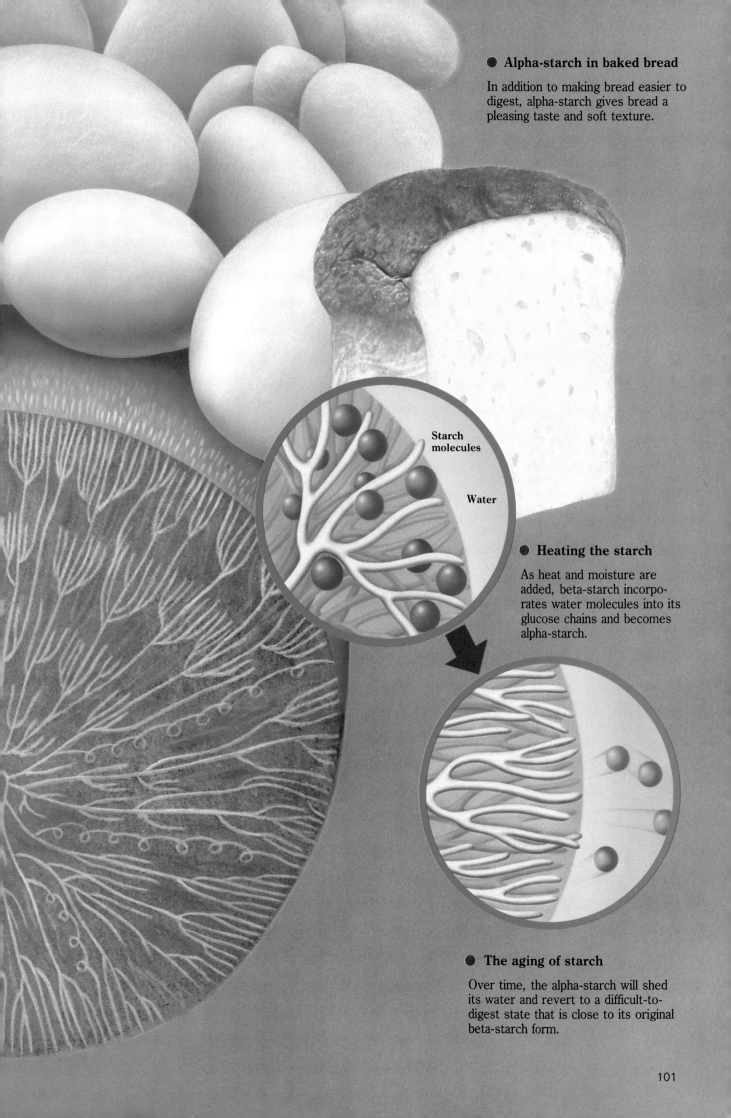

● **Alpha-starch in baked bread**

In addition to making bread easier to digest, alpha-starch gives bread a pleasing taste and soft texture.

Starch
molecules

Water

● **Heating the starch**

As heat and moisture are added, beta-starch incorporates water molecules into its glucose chains and becomes alpha-starch.

● **The aging of starch**

Over time, the alpha-starch will shed its water and revert to a difficult-to-digest state that is close to its original beta-starch form.

5
Engineering a Way of Life

Many advances, both great and small, in the history of civilization were preceded by developments in chemistry. It is no accident, for example, that some of the epochs in human history—such as the Bronze Age and Iron Age—are so named because they marked humanity's improving ability to work metals. In fact, it was the discovery of metal-refining processes that changed the face of civilization from one of small buildings and horse-drawn carts to one of skyscrapers and railroads. Without this breakthrough—as well as the engineering advances in materials such as concrete and glass—there would be no cars, planes, or any of the other technological marvels that people today take for granted.

Complementing the revolution in metals that accompanied the 17th and 18th centuries was the 20th century's revolution in organic chemistry. As engineers discovered the wealth of organic chemicals—that is, chemicals containing carbon—obtainable from the refining of coal and crude oil, a profusion of new products followed. Among them were plastics such as polyethylene and Teflon, as well as synthetic fibers such as nylon and polyester. Furthermore, the large-scale refining of crude oil makes low-cost gasoline and heating oil accessible to almost everyone. In fact, the advances of industrial chemistry so pervade everyday life that it is virtually impossible to pass an entire day without experiencing the wonders of modern chemistry firsthand.

Sparks fly in a blast furnace as carbon reacts with molten iron ore to produce pig iron, an intermediate stage in the production of steel.

How Is Paper Made?

While many fibers such as cotton, linen, and hemp have served as raw materials for paper since writing began about 5,000 years ago, almost all paper today comes from wood. The ingredient that makes wood a good source of paper is a long, fiberlike molecule called cellulose. Along each cellulose molecule lie a number of hydroxyl groups—oxygen atoms bound to hydrogen atoms—that link the strands of cellulose together in a tough mesh.

In the papermaking process, the strands of cellulose are first separated to form pulp. Then the fibers are pressed back together in thin sheets. During pressing, the strands reconnect, forming smooth paper.

Digesting wood

Wood, chopped into matchbook-size chips, goes into a huge tank called a digester. Under great heat and pressure, steam and chemicals free the cellulose from the wood. After a few hours, the wood turns into soft, cottony material called pulp.

Wood chips are the raw material.

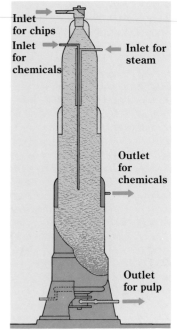

Inlet for chips
Inlet for chemicals
Inlet for steam
Outlet for chemicals
Outlet for pulp

Pressure chamber

5 Winding up the job

The cellulose fibers have become an intertwined mesh *(below)* by the time a large spool called a winder *(bottom)* gathers the finished paper into a giant roll. These rolls are cut into smaller rolls or sheets and shipped from the factory.

4 Final drying on hot rollers

The newly formed paper passes over additional rollers that are heated from within. The hot rollers drive more of the water out of the moving paper.

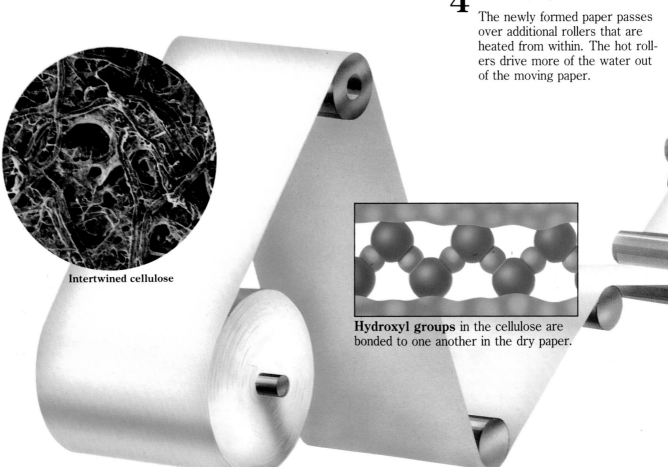

Intertwined cellulose

Hydroxyl groups in the cellulose are bonded to one another in the dry paper.

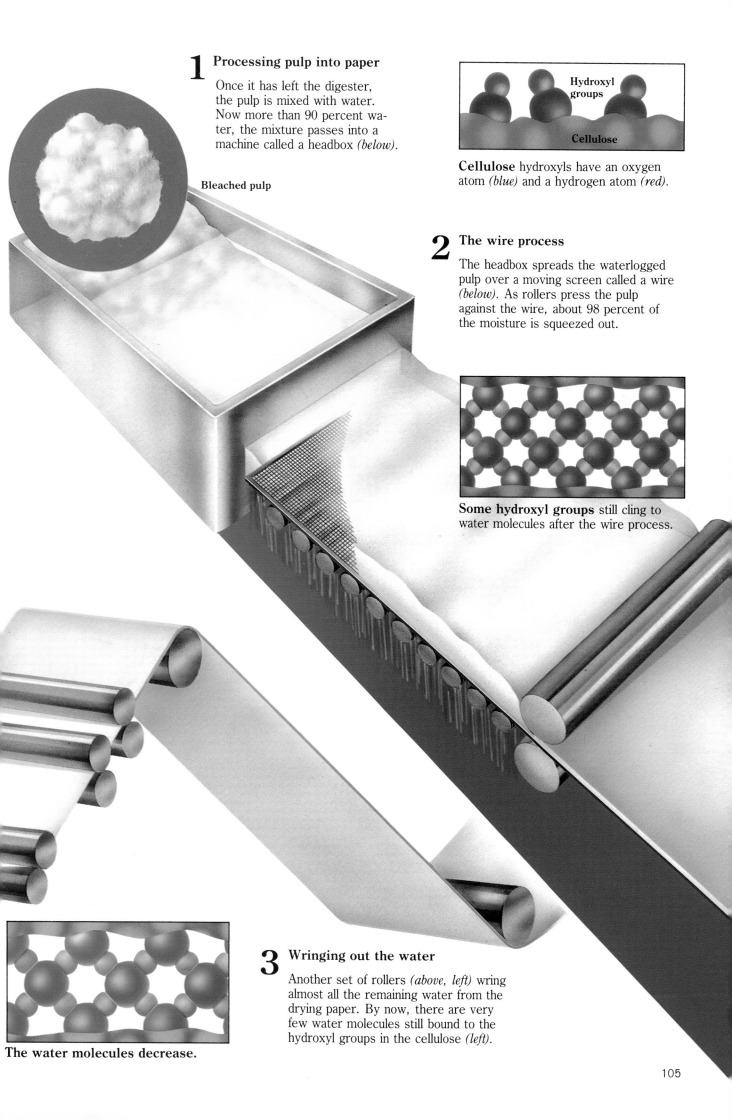

1 Processing pulp into paper

Once it has left the digester, the pulp is mixed with water. Now more than 90 percent water, the mixture passes into a machine called a headbox *(below)*.

Bleached pulp

Cellulose hydroxyls have an oxygen atom *(blue)* and a hydrogen atom *(red)*.

Hydroxyl groups

Cellulose

2 The wire process

The headbox spreads the waterlogged pulp over a moving screen called a wire *(below)*. As rollers press the pulp against the wire, about 98 percent of the moisture is squeezed out.

Some hydroxyl groups still cling to water molecules after the wire process.

3 Wringing out the water

Another set of rollers *(above, left)* wring almost all the remaining water from the drying paper. By now, there are very few water molecules still bound to the hydroxyl groups in the cellulose *(left)*.

The water molecules decrease.

What Are Polymers?

A polymer is a long, chainlike molecule made up of vast numbers of individual molecules joined end to end. Depending on the length of the chain and the molecules used as links, polymers can be made with many different properties. Teflon, for example, is a polymer useful for its slipperiness, while neoprene is valued for its elasticity.

Many polymers occur naturally. Rubber is a natural polymer, as are silk and wool. The human body is full of polymers, from the proteins that make up the body's tissues to the strands of DNA that form the basis for heredity. But many other polymers are artificial. Plastics consist of synthetic polymers that have been molded into various shapes *(pages 118-119)*.

The polymer-making process—illustrated here for polyethylene—is very simple. The monomers—molecules of a chemical to be polymerized, such as ethylene—are fed into a reaction chamber along with a catalyst that promotes the formation of chains. Under high heat and pressure, the monomers forge themselves into a long, regular chain. The length of the chain depends on the reaction time: The longer the monomers stay in the chamber, the longer the polymer chain.

Forging a chemical chain

To make polyethylene—the simplest possible polymer—a large tank is filled with ethylene gas and a catalyst that promotes the linkage of ethylene molecules. Heat and high pressure *(right)* form polymers up to 100,000 atoms long.

Separator

Types of polymers

There are two major types of polymers. In homopolymers, such as polyethylene, the polymer forms from one monomer. Copolymers, such as nylon, are chains in which links alternate between two monomers.

Molecules in single file

The polymerization process breaks one of the two bonds between the carbon atoms in an ethylene molecule. Each carbon atom then links with a carbon atom in another ethylene molecule, forming a long, linear chain.

 Carbon   **Hydrogen**

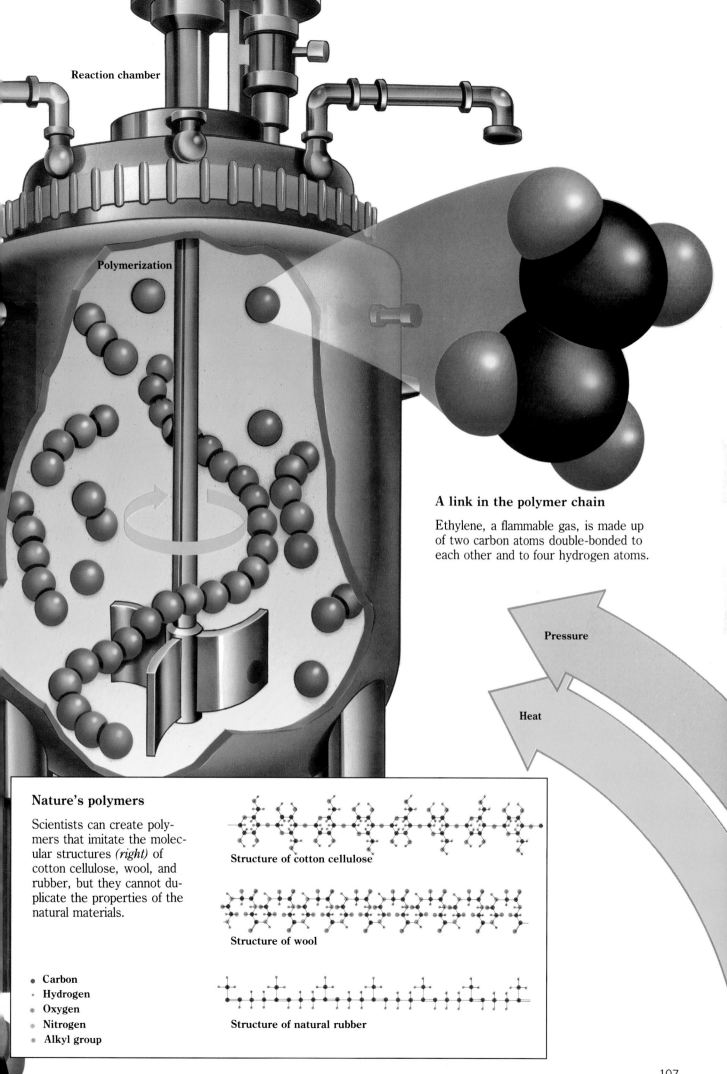

Reaction chamber

Polymerization

A link in the polymer chain

Ethylene, a flammable gas, is made up of two carbon atoms double-bonded to each other and to four hydrogen atoms.

Pressure

Heat

Nature's polymers

Scientists can create polymers that imitate the molecular structures *(right)* of cotton cellulose, wool, and rubber, but they cannot duplicate the properties of the natural materials.

Structure of cotton cellulose

Structure of wool

Structure of natural rubber

- Carbon
- Hydrogen
- Oxygen
- Nitrogen
- Alkyl group

How Are Synthetic Fibers Produced?

One of the most important uses of polymers *(pages 106-107)* is as synthetic fiber. When melted and stretched into threads, polymers can be woven and knitted into fabrics similar to natural materials such as cotton, wool, and silk. The artificial fabrics are often lighter and tougher than their natural counterparts and almost always cheaper to produce.

The first and most famous of synthetic fibers is nylon. Invented by the Du Pont Company in 1930, this remarkable material made its commercial debut in women's stockings but almost immediately also found uses in products ranging from parachutes to fishing line. The triumph of nylon was quickly followed by the invention of other synthetics such as polyester and acrylic, widely used to make clothing.

The most common method for producing synthetic fibers begins with a spinneret *(opposite, top)*. This machine melts polymer chips and forces the melt out through a set of narrow holes. The emerging fibers are wound together to produce a single thread, which is woven with similar threads into bolts of fabric.

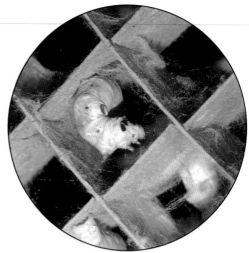

Silkworms produce silk, one of the world's most prized natural fibers. The larva spins fine filaments from an organ in its mouth.

Molecular structure of silk

Molecular structure of nylon

Cooling and stretching

As the fiber cools, it is "drawn," pulled off one spool and onto another that turns four times as fast. Drawing stretches the yarn and strengthens it by making the long molecules fall into parallel bundles.

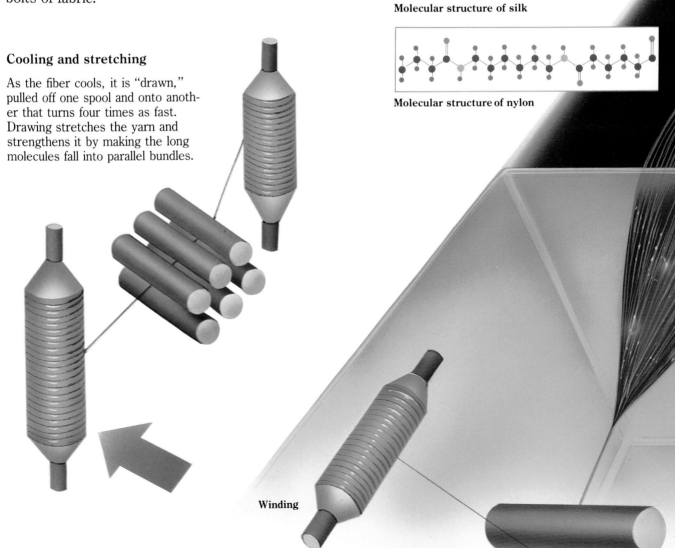

Winding

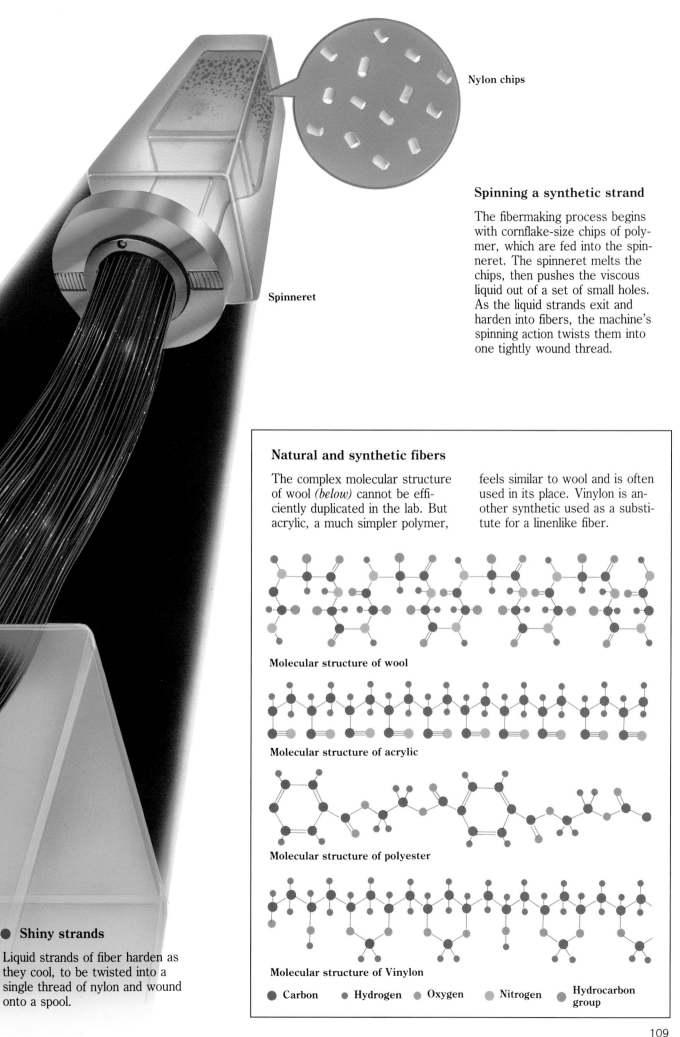

Nylon chips

Spinneret

Spinning a synthetic strand

The fibermaking process begins with cornflake-size chips of polymer, which are fed into the spinneret. The spinneret melts the chips, then pushes the viscous liquid out of a set of small holes. As the liquid strands exit and harden into fibers, the machine's spinning action twists them into one tightly wound thread.

Shiny strands

Liquid strands of fiber harden as they cool, to be twisted into a single thread of nylon and wound onto a spool.

Natural and synthetic fibers

The complex molecular structure of wool *(below)* cannot be efficiently duplicated in the lab. But acrylic, a much simpler polymer, feels similar to wool and is often used in its place. Vinylon is another synthetic used as a substitute for a linenlike fiber.

Molecular structure of wool

Molecular structure of acrylic

Molecular structure of polyester

Molecular structure of Vinylon

● Carbon ● Hydrogen ● Oxygen ● Nitrogen ● Hydrocarbon group

How Is Metal Extracted from Ore?

Most metals do not naturally occur in their pure state. Rather, they exist as ores in which the metal has oxidized, or given up some of its electrons to the oxygen or the other atoms with which it is bound. Iron, for example, tends to surrender electrons to oxygen, creating iron oxide ore. To extract pure iron from iron ore, or to release any other metal from its ore, the metal must regain its electrons in a reduction.

The processes for reducing ores vary with different metals. For iron oxides, one method called indirect reduction involves mixing the ore with coke—coal processed to contain mostly carbon—and limestone in a fiery chamber called a blast furnace *(right)*. Reduction, as shown on these pages, causes molten iron to separate out to be collected. Copper refining involves forcing air or hydrogen gas through molten ore; this is known as smelting.

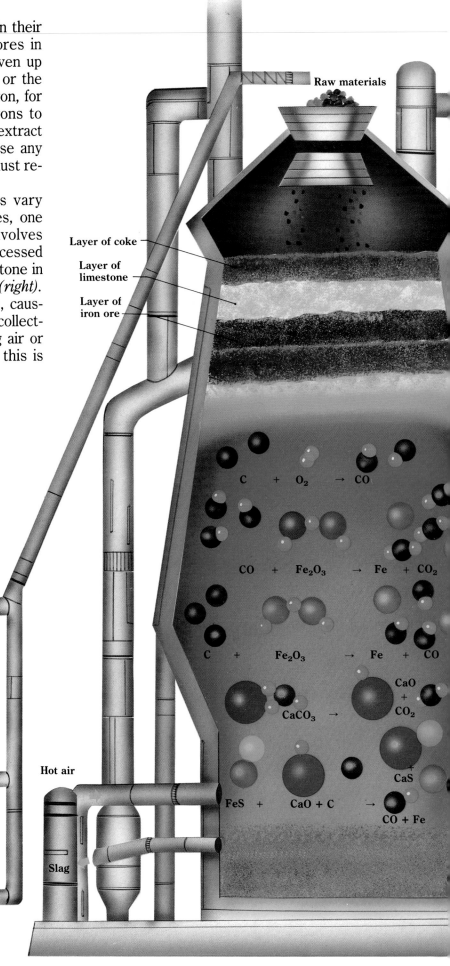

Raw materials

Layer of coke

Layer of limestone

Layer of iron ore

$$C + O_2 \rightarrow CO$$

$$CO + Fe_2O_3 \rightarrow Fe + CO_2$$

$$C + Fe_2O_3 \rightarrow Fe + CO$$

$$CaCO_3 \rightarrow CaO + CO_2$$

$$FeS + CaO + C \rightarrow CaS + CO + Fe$$

Hot air

Slag

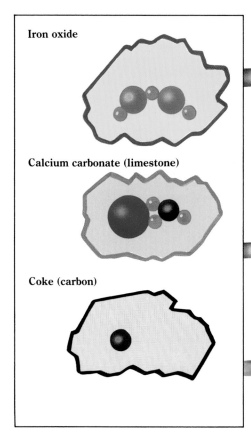

Iron oxide

Calcium carbonate (limestone)

Coke (carbon)

Gaining and losing electrons

Like iron, copper is an important metal usually found as an ore. In copper oxide *(right)* the copper has bonded to oxygen *(blue)*. When exposed to hydrogen gas, the copper oxide is reduced—it loses the oxygen and becomes pure copper. The oxygen combines with the hydrogen, forming water.

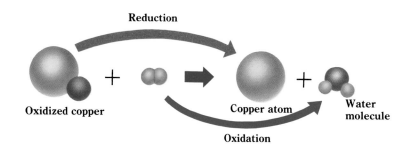

Reduction

Oxidized copper + → Copper atom + Water molecule

Oxidation

Refining iron

Coke burns in the blast of hot air rushing into the furnace. In the flames, the coke's carbon combines with oxygen to produce carbon monoxide.

Carbon monoxide removes oxygen from the iron oxide by indirect reduction. The carbon monoxide gains one oxygen atom to become carbon dioxide, leaving behind raw iron.

In a separate reaction, carbon from the coke takes oxygen from the iron oxide, forming carbon monoxide and raw iron.

Impurities in the ore and the limestone's calcium form slag, or calcium sulfide. The slag and the iron are drawn from the furnace separately. The raw iron goes to the converter.

C = Carbon
O_2 = Oxygen molecule
CO = Carbon monoxide
CO_2 = Carbon dioxide
Fe = Iron
Fe_2O_3 = Iron oxide
FeS = Ferrous sulfide
$CaCO_3$ = Calcium carbonate
CaO = Calcium oxide
CaS = Calcium sulfide

Hot air

Refining copper

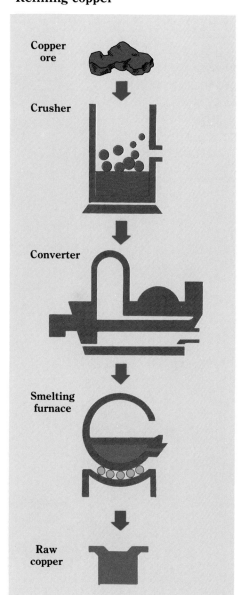

Copper ore

Crusher

Converter

Smelting furnace

Raw copper

Ore rich in copper is pulverized and suspended in water. The copper sulfide in the ore is then extracted.

A converter exposes copper sulfide to air. The sulfur and oxygen form sulfur dioxide gas, leaving raw copper.

The raw copper melts in a smelting furnace, and the molten copper is drained off.

The copper, which is more than 99 percent pure, is further refined in an electrolysis tank *(pages 114-115).*

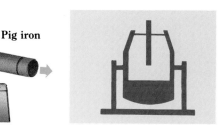

Pig iron

The converter

In the converter, oxygen blown through the raw, or pig, iron removes carbon, leaving carbon dioxide and low-carbon iron, or steel.

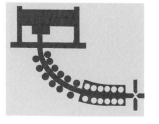

The finish

Steel is cast into plates, after which it is ready to be rolled, cut, and molded into desired shapes, such as sheets or pipes.

Why Are Alloys Used?

An alloy is a metal that contains small amounts of other elements. The presence of these extra elements—either metals or nonmetals—alters the natural properties of the metal, making it stronger, more resilient, or easier to work with. While many alloys enjoy widespread industrial and domestic use, one of the most important alloys is steel, a combination of iron and carbon.

Refining iron *(pages 110-111)* first produces pig iron, which contains a great deal of carbon. This high carbon content renders pig iron too brittle for many uses, but removing some of the carbon makes the steel easier to work. This is done by passing a stream of oxygen over a container of molten pig iron. By controlling the amount of oxygen released, engineers produce steel with precise amounts of carbon.

Casting pig iron

Pig iron's high carbon content makes it brittle and difficult to work. Its only important use is for casting, in which molten pig iron *(below)* is poured into a mold and cooled.

Converting pig iron

In a converter *(below),* oxygen removes carbon from pig iron by combining with the carbon and escaping as carbon monoxide.

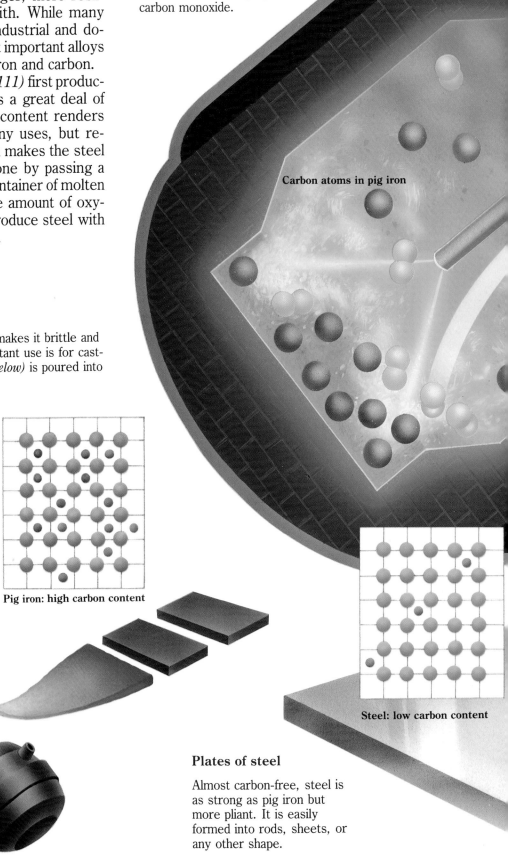

Carbon atoms in pig iron

Pig iron: high carbon content

Steel: low carbon content

Blast furnace

Converter

Plates of steel

Almost carbon-free, steel is as strong as pig iron but more pliant. It is easily formed into rods, sheets, or any other shape.

112

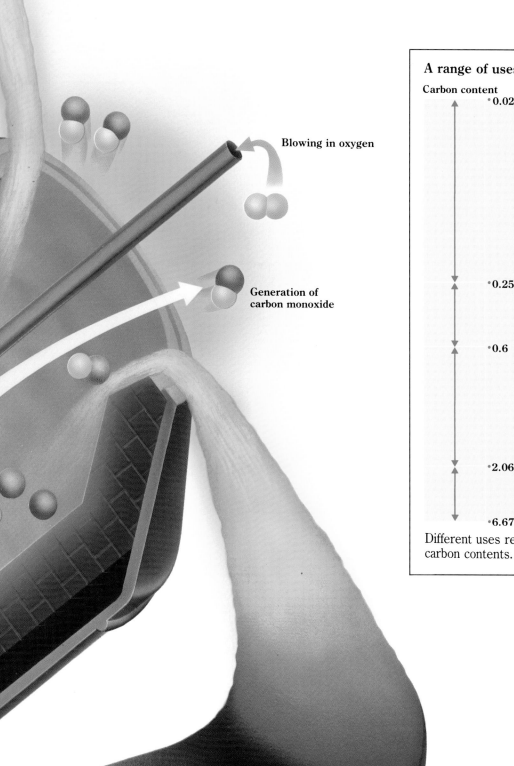

Blowing in oxygen

Generation of carbon monoxide

A range of uses for steel

Carbon content

$\cdot 0.02\,(\%)$

Low-carbon steel

Wire

Nails

Galvanized sheet iron

Tin plate

$\cdot 0.25$ Medium-carbon steel

Structural materials for automobiles, ships, bridges, and other structures

$\cdot 0.6$

High-carbon steel

Saws

Cutlery

$\cdot 2.06$

Cast iron

Cast-iron materials

$\cdot 6.67$

Different uses require steel with varying carbon contents.

Other iron alloys

Besides carbon, small amounts of metals also impart useful properties to steel. The addition of chromium, for example, produces a corrosion-resistant alloy called stainless steel. Adding a trace of tungsten creates high-speed steel, a tough alloy used to make grinding equipment.

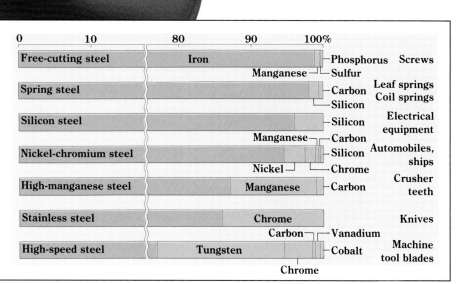

	0	10	80	90	100%	
Free-cutting steel		Iron				Phosphorus — Screws / Sulfur / Manganese
Spring steel						Carbon — Leaf springs, Coil springs / Silicon
Silicon steel						Silicon — Electrical equipment
Nickel-chromium steel						Manganese — Carbon / Silicon — Automobiles, ships / Nickel — Chrome
High-manganese steel			Manganese			Carbon — Crusher teeth
Stainless steel			Chrome			Knives
High-speed steel		Tungsten				Carbon — Vanadium / Cobalt — Machine tool blades / Chrome

How Are Copper and Aluminum Refined?

The industrial refining of copper and aluminum uses a technique called electrolysis, in which an electric current separates a metal from other elements. For aluminum, the process begins with aluminum oxide, or alumina. This ore goes into a tank with an electrically conducting solution and two electrodes. A carbon plate serves as one electrode; the bottom of the tank acts as the other. Under an electric current the aluminum reduces, melts, and sinks to the bottom of the tank. At the same time, the alumina's oxygen binds to the carbon electrode and bubbles off as carbon dioxide.

Copper refining starts with ores, which are reduced in a blast furnace to nearly pure metal. A block of raw copper serves as one electrode in the electrolysis tank, while a pure copper plate is the other. When the current is turned on, the copper in the impure electrode reduces and migrates to the pure electrode, leaving the impurities behind.

Copper in the rough

Copper ore—a mixture of copper oxides, sulfides, or carbonates *(below)*—is refined in a blast furnace to raw, impure copper before it is suitable for electrolysis.

Copper ore

A copper-refining circuit

As copper ions migrate under an electric current, the electrode of impure copper *(below, right)* disintegrates, and the pure electrode grows larger.

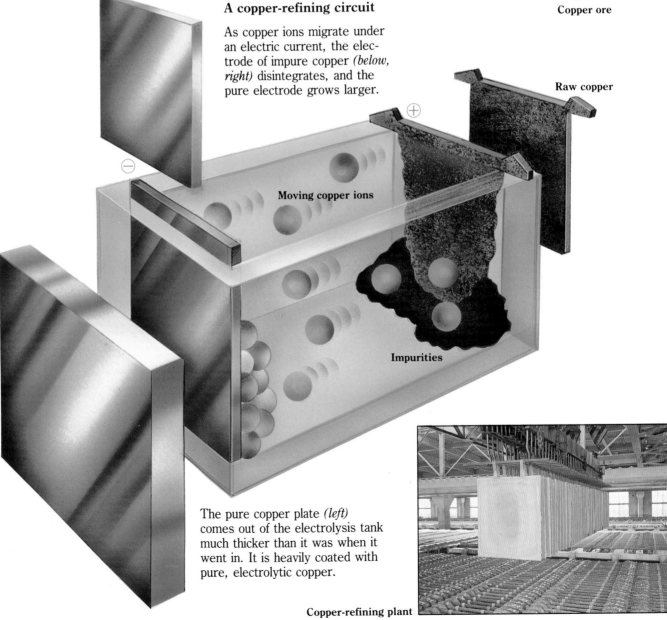

Raw copper

Moving copper ions

Impurities

The pure copper plate *(left)* comes out of the electrolysis tank much thicker than it was when it went in. It is heavily coated with pure, electrolytic copper.

Copper-refining plant

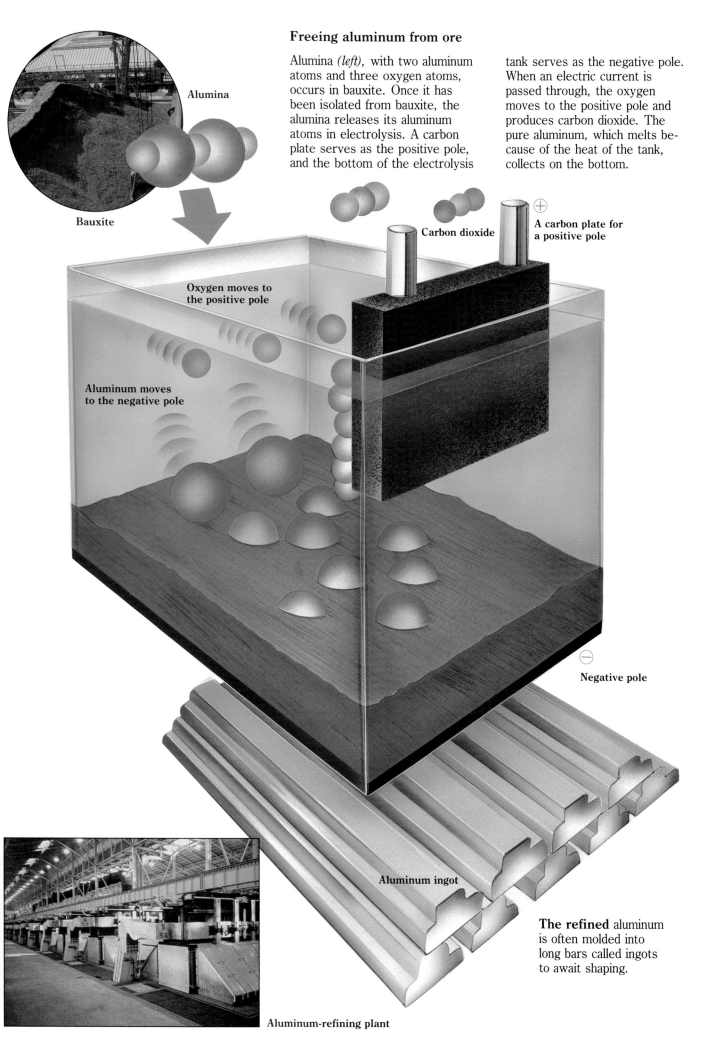

Freeing aluminum from ore

Alumina *(left),* with two aluminum atoms and three oxygen atoms, occurs in bauxite. Once it has been isolated from bauxite, the alumina releases its aluminum atoms in electrolysis. A carbon plate serves as the positive pole, and the bottom of the electrolysis tank serves as the negative pole. When an electric current is passed through, the oxygen moves to the positive pole and produces carbon dioxide. The pure aluminum, which melts because of the heat of the tank, collects on the bottom.

Alumina

Bauxite

Carbon dioxide

A carbon plate for a positive pole

Oxygen moves to the positive pole

Aluminum moves to the negative pole

Negative pole

Aluminum ingot

The refined aluminum is often molded into long bars called ingots to await shaping.

Aluminum-refining plant

115

How Does Crude Oil Become Gasoline?

Crude oil pumped from the ground contains many different types of hydrocarbon molecules, each with its own chemical properties and commercial uses. Some of the smaller molecules are converted into gasoline, the larger ones into heating oil. But first the components—called fractions—must be separated.

Oil refineries use a separation technique known as fractional distillation, which exploits the fact that the different fractions condense at different temperatures. The process begins as the crude oil is heated *(below)* to 400° C., or 750° F., a temperature high enough to vaporize about half the oil. The vapor rises through a tall multilevel structure called a fractionating tower *(right)*, cooling as it works its way up. As each fraction reaches the temperature level at which it condenses, it drips into a collecting shelf *(blue outlines)*. The remaining vapor continues upward, condensing out fraction by fraction. The residue that did not vaporize at the first heating is called heavy oil and is used to make asphalt and heavy fuel oil.

The refining process

Mushroom-shaped "bubble caps" lie across the vents between collecting shelves. As the vapor rises, it lifts the caps and flows out.

A heating furnace starts the distillation by vaporizing the volatile crude oil, which is a mixture of fractions, each with its own properties.

The fractionating tower collects the separated fractions as they condense out of the rising, cooling vapor.

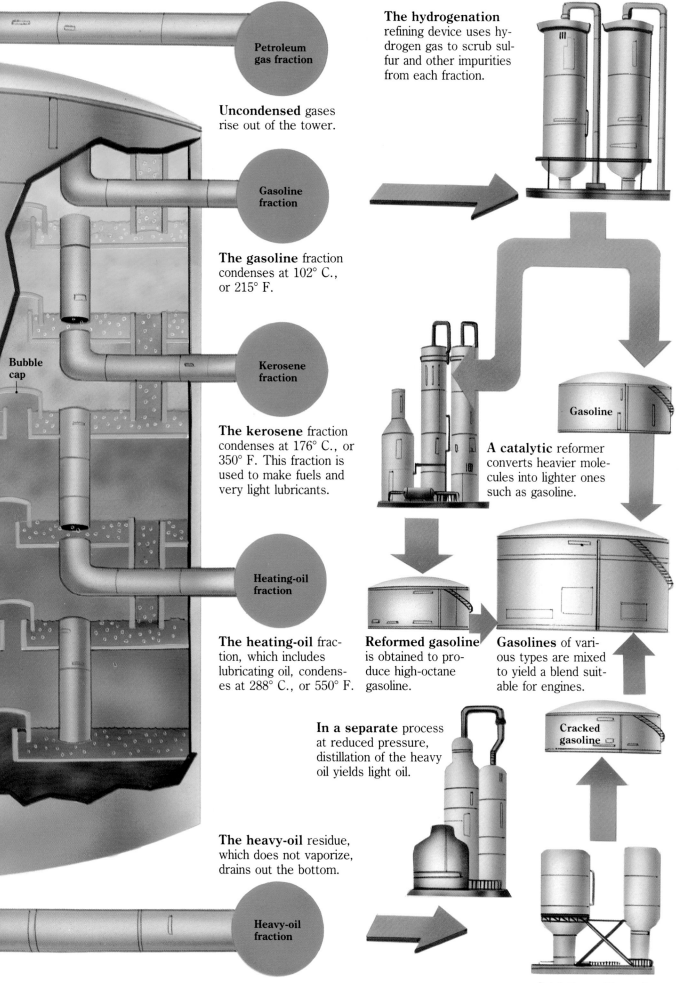

Petroleum gas fraction

Uncondensed gases rise out of the tower.

The hydrogenation refining device uses hydrogen gas to scrub sulfur and other impurities from each fraction.

Gasoline fraction

The gasoline fraction condenses at 102° C., or 215° F.

Kerosene fraction

The kerosene fraction condenses at 176° C., or 350° F. This fraction is used to make fuels and very light lubricants.

Bubble cap

Heating-oil fraction

The heating-oil fraction, which includes lubricating oil, condenses at 288° C., or 550° F.

Gasoline

A catalytic reformer converts heavier molecules into lighter ones such as gasoline.

Reformed gasoline is obtained to produce high-octane gasoline.

Gasolines of various types are mixed to yield a blend suitable for engines.

In a separate process at reduced pressure, distillation of the heavy oil yields light oil.

The heavy-oil residue, which does not vaporize, drains out the bottom.

Cracked gasoline

Heavy-oil fraction

Catalytic cracking unit

117

How Were Plastics Developed?

Like synthetic fibers, plastics are made from polymers. But rather than being spun into strands, these polymers—called resins—are melted down and molded into the desired shape. Many different resins are available for this purpose, allowing manufacturers to produce plastics with a great range of properties.

Engineers identify two kinds of plastics. The first type, known as thermoplastic resins, are very hard but become pliant when heated. Such plastics, which include polyethylene and most polyesters, are shaped through a technique called injection molding. In this process, a machine melts pellets of the desired resin and shoots the melt into a mold.

The other plastics are the thermosetting resins. Once heated above a certain temperature, their molecular structures change and these resins become very hard. Not even additional heating will soften them once this transformation has occurred. The process for shaping these plastics, called compression molding, involves filling a mold with powdered resin and heating it until the resin hardens.

Methods of molding plastics

Thermoplastic resins

Rigid at room temperature, a thermoplastic resin softens and is easy to mold every time it is heated.

Ingredients in pellet form

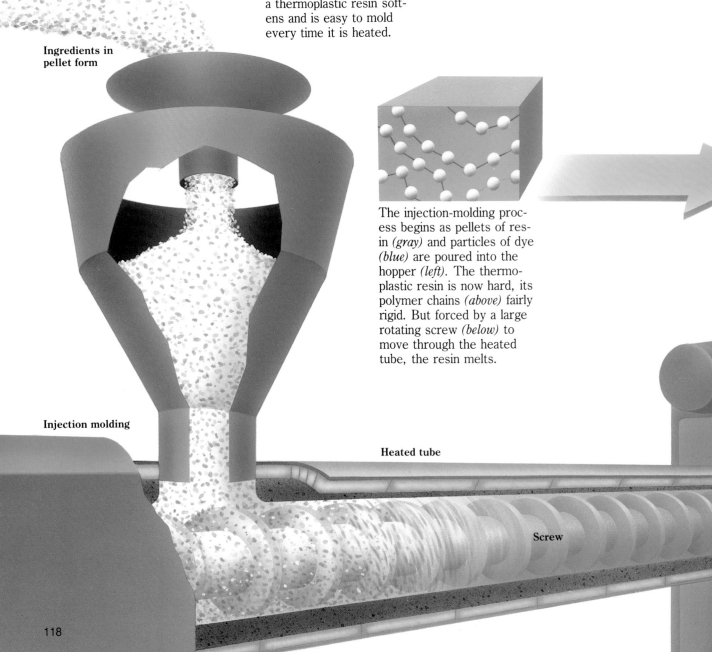

The injection-molding process begins as pellets of resin *(gray)* and particles of dye *(blue)* are poured into the hopper *(left)*. The thermoplastic resin is now hard, its polymer chains *(above)* fairly rigid. But forced by a large rotating screw *(below)* to move through the heated tube, the resin melts.

Injection molding

Heated tube

Screw

Compression molding

Ingredients in powdered form

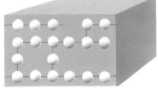

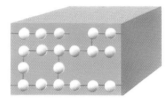

Thermosetting resin polymers resemble those in thermoplastic resins, but their chains are shorter.

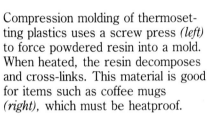

When heated under high pressure, polymer chains cross-link, forming bonds in a tough molecular mesh.

Once it has formed, the polymer network holds even if reheated.

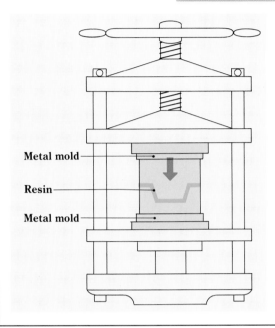

Metal mold

Resin

Metal mold

Compression molding of thermosetting plastics uses a screw press *(left)* to force powdered resin into a mold. When heated, the resin decomposes and cross-links. This material is good for items such as coffee mugs *(right)*, which must be heatproof.

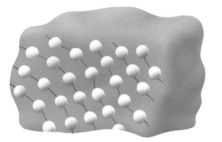

The melted resin is injected into the mold *(below)*. The heat makes the polymer chains *(above)* lose their rigidity and slide past one another.

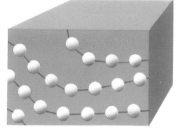

Once molded into the desired shape *(below)* and cooled, the polymers reassume their rigid configuration *(above)* and the plastic solidifies.

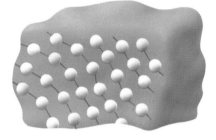

Reheated, a thermoplastic resin returns to the fluid state *(above)*. On each reheating, the molded object *(below)* melts and becomes pliable.

Metal mold

Thermoplastic products such as the trash can above lose their shape if heated.

The injection-molding machine melts the resin and dye together, and a rotating screw forces the melt into a mold. The product—here, a trash can—is unmolded only after cooling and hardening.

What Makes Concrete Harden?

Concrete consists of three ingredients. The first is cement, a fine powder of various minerals. The second is aggregate, a mixture of rocky particles ranging in size from gravel to sand. The third is water, which is essential for the concrete to set.

When water is added to the first two ingredients, it reacts chemically with minerals in the cement, forming a highly adhesive compound that surrounds and sticks to the aggregate particles. Over the next several hours, this paste then stiffens into a stonelike material in a process called setting, or curing. The water does not evaporate from the cement, rather it becomes bonded within it in new compounds. The result is a hard, strong material used in buildings, bridges, roads, and countless other structures large and small.

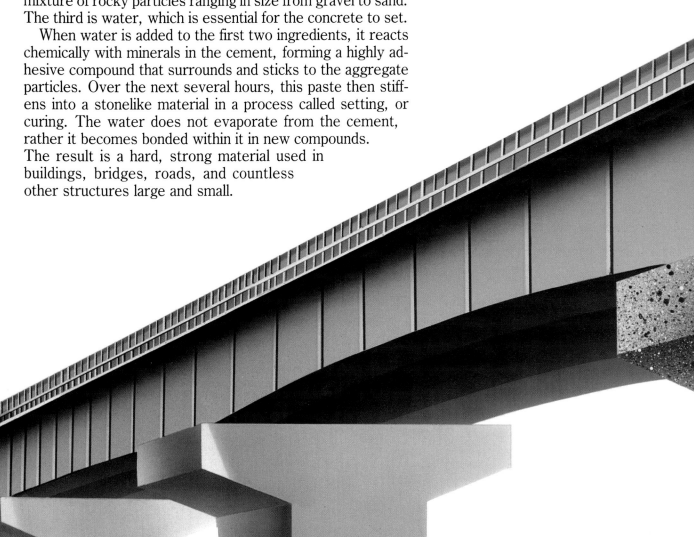

Connecting concrete with water

When water is mixed into cement, hydration occurs as water molecules transform cement particles into new adhesive compounds. The hydrated cement surrounds the aggregate particles *(below, third from left)* and hardens. For maximum strength, the hydrated cement must pack the spaces *(below, right)*.

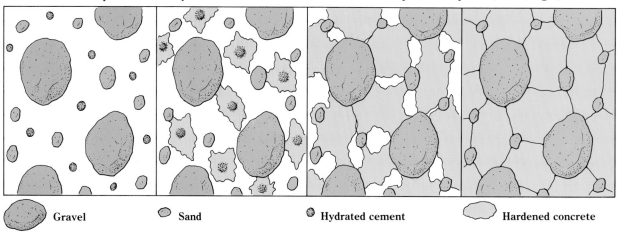

| ⬤ Gravel | ○ Sand | ⦿ Hydrated cement | ⬡ Hardened concrete |

Metal atoms

The structure of a metal

In metallic crystals *(above, left)*, metal atoms *(above)* pack tightly together in a strong, symmetric lattice in which each atom pulls on those around it.

▲ Concrete

Cement

Sand

Gravel

The structure of concrete

Concrete forms a compact lattice much like metal's. Each particle of cement pulls at its neighboring pieces of sand and gravel. This reinforcement makes concrete a good partner for metal in supporting a bridge or other heavy load.

How Is Glass Shaped?

Most glass is made from a mixture of soda and lime and silicon dioxide, the main ingredient of sand. In sand, silicon dioxide forms long, fairly regular networks of silicon and oxygen atoms. These networks lose their coherence when the raw materials are melted, but they quickly fall back into lockstep when cooled. To make glass, however, the melt is cooled too quickly for this molecular realignment to occur. Instead the molecules stick where they are, forming disorganized networks that are no longer liquid, yet neither are the links the crystalline lattices characteristic of true solids.

Most of the glass manufactured is plate glass, used in doors and windows everywhere. One of the techniques for making this glass is illustrated below. In this process, silicon dioxide is first melted and mixed with other ingredients. The mix then flows down a trough and is fed into a set of rollers that press it into a thin sheet.

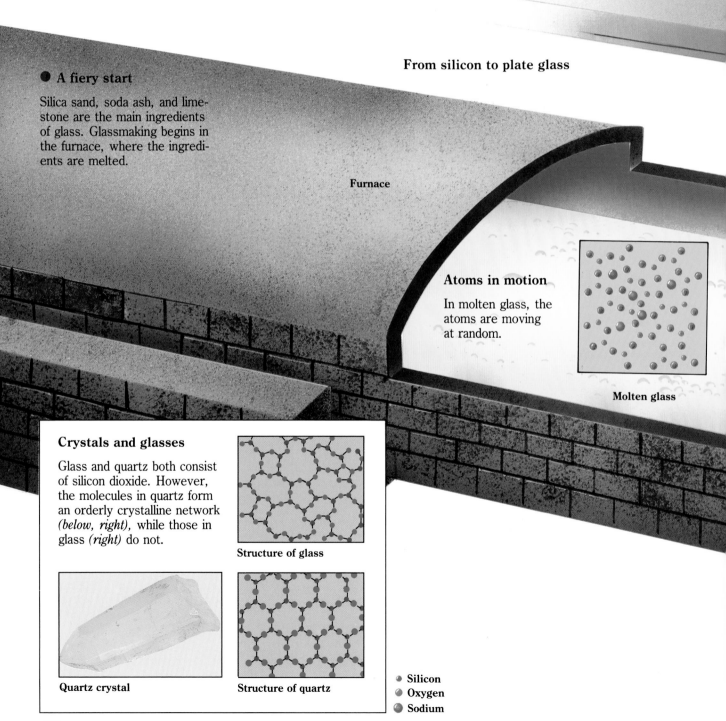

From silicon to plate glass

● **A fiery start**

Silica sand, soda ash, and lime-stone are the main ingredients of glass. Glassmaking begins in the furnace, where the ingredients are melted.

Furnace

Atoms in motion

In molten glass, the atoms are moving at random.

Molten glass

Crystals and glasses

Glass and quartz both consist of silicon dioxide. However, the molecules in quartz form an orderly crystalline network *(below, right)*, while those in glass *(right)* do not.

Structure of glass

Quartz crystal

Structure of quartz

● Silicon
● Oxygen
● Sodium

122

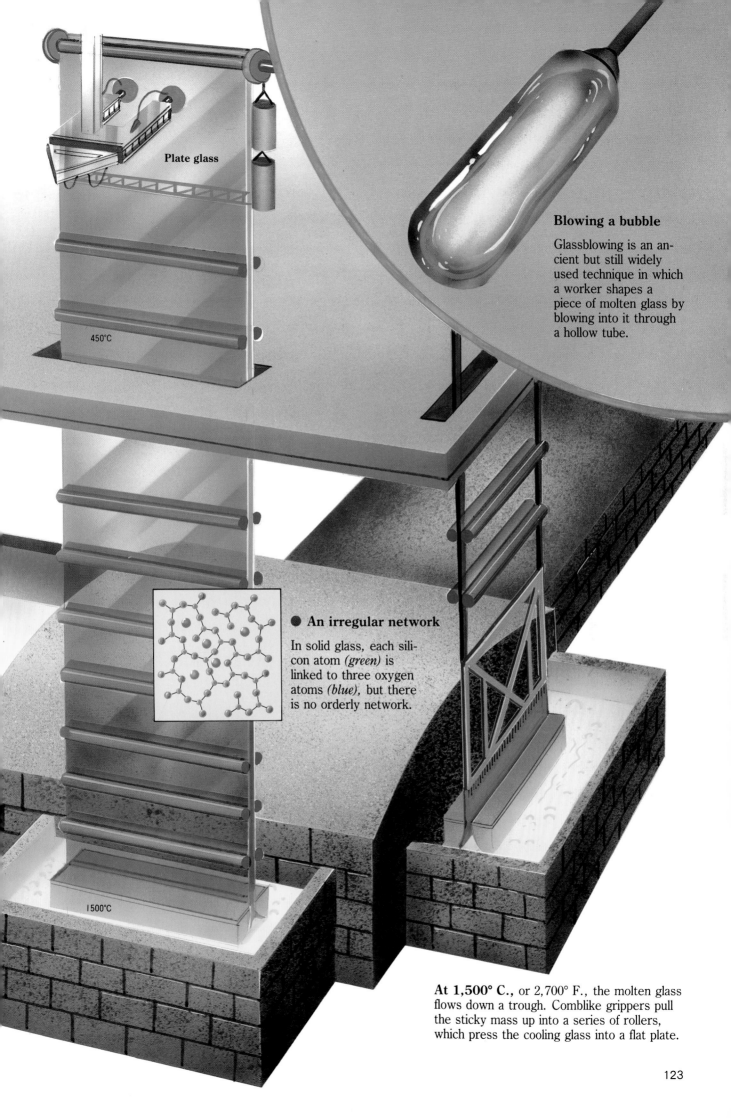

Plate glass

450°C

Blowing a bubble

Glassblowing is an ancient but still widely used technique in which a worker shapes a piece of molten glass by blowing into it through a hollow tube.

● **An irregular network**

In solid glass, each silicon atom *(green)* is linked to three oxygen atoms *(blue)*, but there is no orderly network.

1500°C

At 1,500° C., or 2,700° F., the molten glass flows down a trough. Comblike grippers pull the sticky mass up into a series of rollers, which press the cooling glass into a flat plate.

What Are Some Uses for Glass?

Glass is an extraordinary substance. Its chief ingredient—silicon dioxide—is one of the cheapest, most plentiful materials on Earth. Yet glass has remarkable properties and myriad uses, not only in windows and glassware but also in less obvious places such as insulating fibers and communications cables. One glass company has developed 100,000 kinds of glass.

The key to the versatility of glass lies in the fact that tiny alterations in the ingredients list or the manufacturing method can drastically change its physical properties. Examples of special kinds of glass on these pages include borosilicate glass—so heat-resistant it is used for cooking vessels—and tempered safety glass, which holds together when broken so that shattered windshields shower car crash victims with tiny cubes of glass rather than with lethal flying shards.

Sending a signal through glass

An optical fiber *(above, right)* has two parts: a glass core and a surrounding glass layer called the cladding. Confined by the cladding, coded pulses of light race through the core over long distances. Large numbers of fibers bound together *(below)* form an optical cable, which can carry far more information than a metal cable of the same size. To make a single optical fiber *(left)*, molten glass forming the core *(purple)* is forced out the bottom of a second pool of molten glass *(green)*, giving the core a coating, which is the cladding.

Furnace   Furnace

Core

Cladding

Optical-fiber cable

Spinning a glass fiber

A glass-spinning machine *(below)* pushes molten glass through tiny holes, producing thin threads, then spins them into a tough, flexible fiber. A similar method is used to make synthetic fibers *(pages 108-109)*.

Ingredients

Furnace

Glass

Production process   Glass fiber

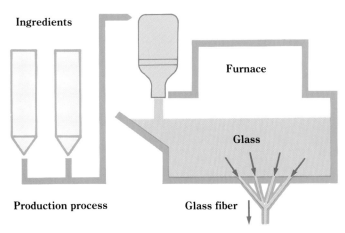

Glass fibers can be spun into yarns *(above, left)* or blended with plastic and loosely packed as insulating material.

Heat-insulating material

Light bounces through an optical fiber between core and cladding.

Boron-enhanced glass

Boron oxide in the melt yields hard, heat-resistant glass, ideal for laboratory equipment.

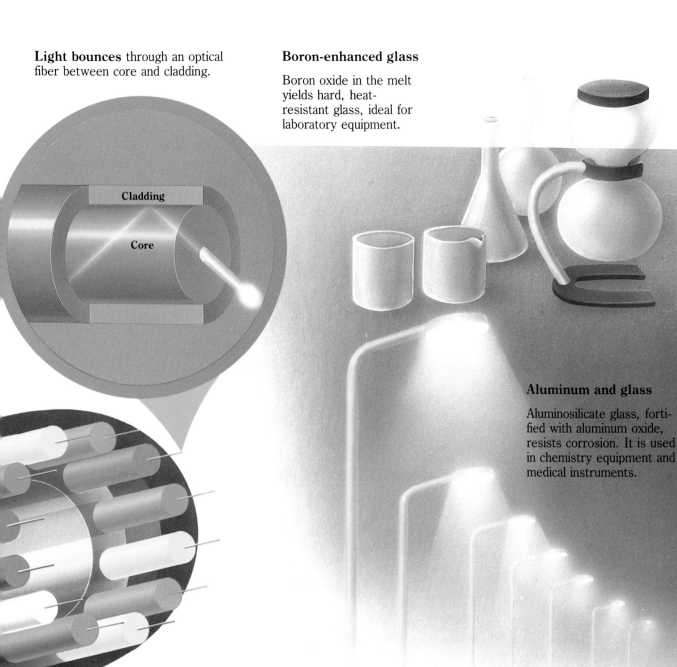

Cladding

Core

Aluminum and glass

Aluminosilicate glass, fortified with aluminum oxide, resists corrosion. It is used in chemistry equipment and medical instruments.

Tempered safety glass

Safety glass is given a special heat treatment. Used in doors and car windows, it prevents many serious injuries because it breaks into small, dull-edged fragments.

Leaded glass

Lead oxide gives crystal glassware *(below)* its distinctive luster. The glass is also used to manufacture lenses and prisms.

Cameras use leaded-glass lenses.

How Is Perfume Made?

Used since the dawn of recorded history, perfumes are pleasant-smelling solutions of aromatic chemicals. To be aromatic—that is, detectable by the human nose—a substance needs special qualities. Its molecules must be light enough to float on air and reach the nose, and they must be water-soluble to let them enter the olfactory gland and be transmitted to the receptor cells in the brain. Extracting naturally fragrant substances without destroying their complex chemical characteristics calls for careful handling indeed.

The most widely used methods for extracting fragrance from flowers such as the rose petals shown here are solvent extraction *(below)* and steam distillation *(right)*. In solvent extraction, the flowers are soaked in a liquid that dissolves the aromatic molecules. The solids are then filtered out and the solvent evaporated, leaving the desired oil. In steam distillation, steam takes the fragrant oils from the flowers to a condenser, where the steam condenses into water and separates from the oil.

Obtaining the essence

Vapor pressure from steam induces the fragrant oils in flower petals to vaporize at temperatures lower than their boiling points. This lets technicians extract the oils without damage.

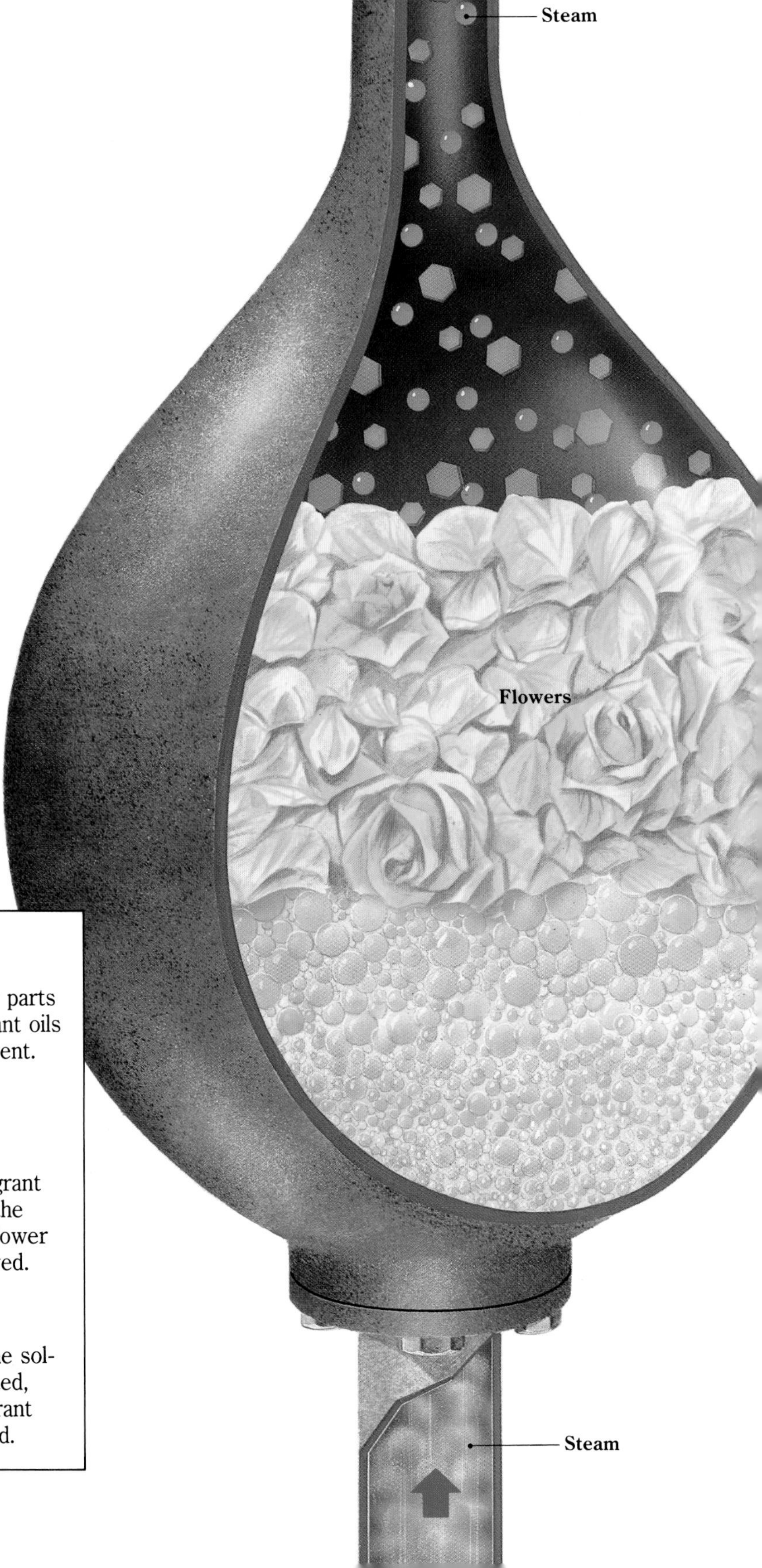

Fragrant substances

Steam

Flowers

Steam

Solvent extraction

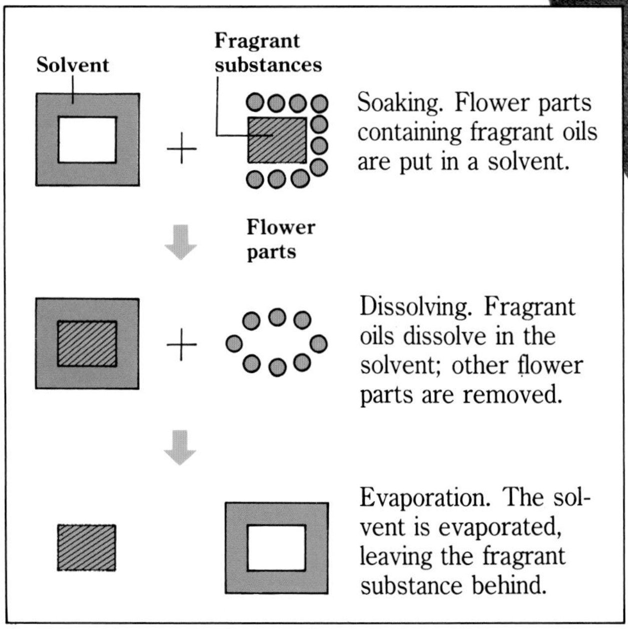

Solvent

Fragrant substances

Soaking. Flower parts containing fragrant oils are put in a solvent.

Flower parts

Dissolving. Fragrant oils dissolve in the solvent; other flower parts are removed.

Evaporation. The solvent is evaporated, leaving the fragrant substance behind.

126

Capturing the fragrance

As the fragrant molecules evaporate, they travel with the steam to a condenser. There, the steam reverts to water, and the fragrant vapors become oils again.

Oil and water

As the oil and water condense, they drip into a containing vessel and separate out. The water sinks to the bottom, while the lighter oils collect at the top.

Fragrant oils

Water

Alcohol
Fragrant substances

The finished product

The oils are combined to produce the desired scent, then dissolved in alcohol. As alcohol *(triangles)* evaporates, it carries fragrance with it.

6
Exploring the New Materials

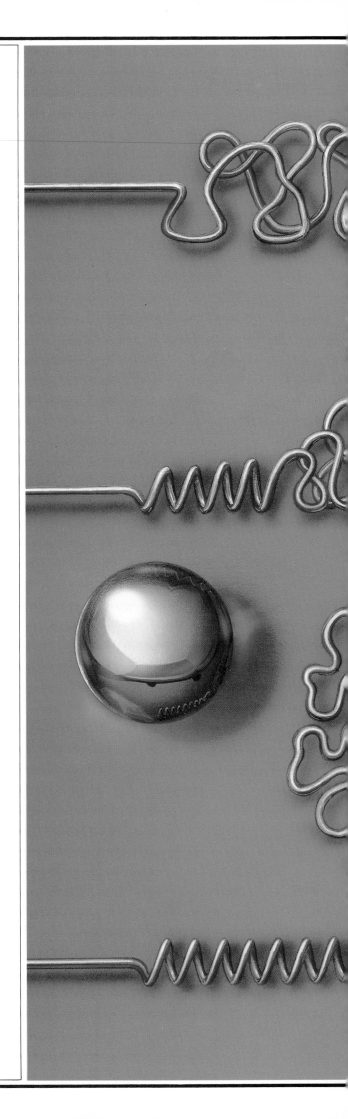

Ever since the first potters turned pliable earth into hardened ceramics some 10,000 years ago, people have been looking for ways to transform natural materials into new substances. In the late 1800s experiments produced the first synthetic organic compounds, but since the 1950s scientists have produced truly revolutionary materials custom-engineered to meet specific technical or industrial needs.

Behind these advances is the new science of materials technology. Its practitioners, aided by supermagnifying electron microscopes and specialized processing techniques, have learned to alter a material's atomic structure and hence its characteristics—traits such as how hard or elastic it is or how well it withstands heat. Research has produced a whole range of synthetic materials that are transforming every facet of modern life. Tough, wear-resistant ceramics serve as artificial bone implants or blades that cut steel, while millions of winking liquid-crystal molecules form color images on pocket-size television screens. In the auto industry, tough, lightweight parts made of carbon fiber-reinforced plastics make vehicles lighter so they run on less fuel.

These are only a few of the more common applications for today's advanced materials. Chemists working with the structure of matter are constantly developing new ones. This chapter will look at some of the advanced materials currently in use.

Among the marvels of today's advanced materials are shape-memory alloys—metallic solids that "remember" their initial form. At right, shape-memory wire twisted into a tangle *(top)* gradually resumes its original shape *(bottom)* when heated.

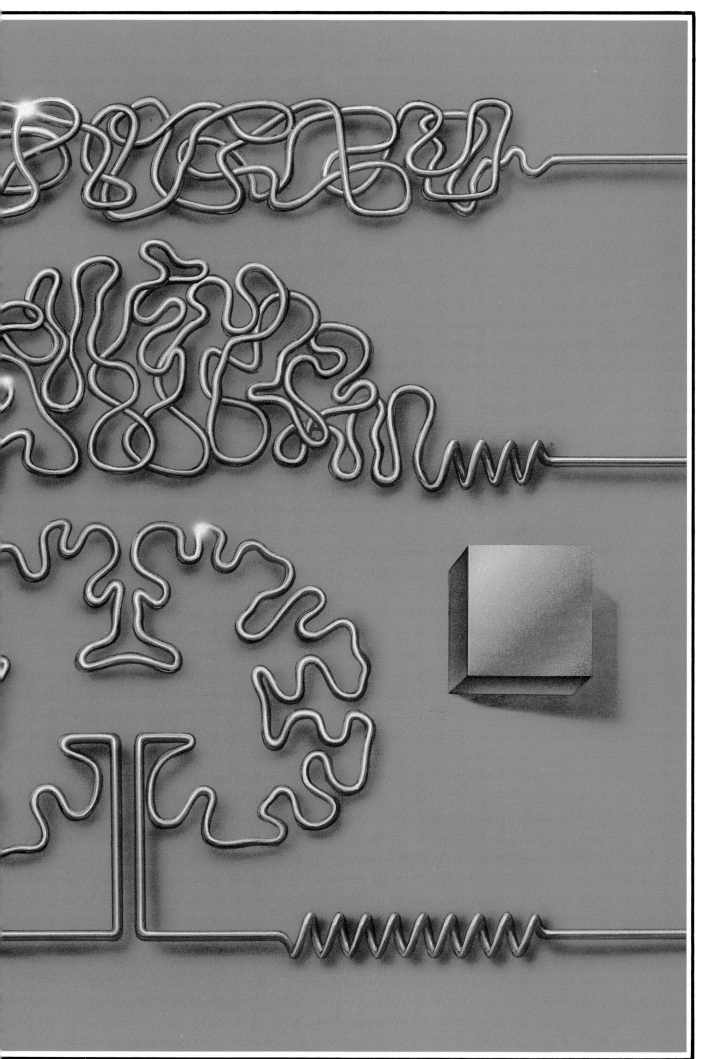

What Are Advanced Ceramics?

The word *ceramics* comes from a Greek word meaning "earthenware." In traditional ceramics—pottery, brick, porcelain, and glass—the essential ingredient is clay. The clay particles, together with other minerals, are fused by heat, so that their atoms bond together. The bonded atoms are sometimes grouped into orderly, three-dimensional arrays known as crystals. In many ceramics, the crystals form large groups of linked crystals called polycrystalline grains. The structure of these grains determines the toughness, porosity, and melting point of a ceramic material.

Advanced ceramics produced by new chemical methods are fused by heat, as traditional ceramics are. But new ceramics technology provides custom-made materials for things as different as artificial knee joints and engine turbochargers. These new ceramic materials combine great strength, heat resistance, hardness, and chemical stability—properties that depend on the materials' atomic arrangement. Chemical engineers manipulate a ceramic's atomic arrangement by carefully controlling the purity, mix, and fineness of the ingredients, and the amount of heat used in firing. In this way, they make new materials with properties tailored to specific uses.

Ceramics that slice through metal

Unlike metal cutting tools, blades fashioned from advanced ceramics cut through iron without overheating or dulling. Such wear resistance results from the strong chemical bonds linking the atoms in the ceramic blade.

Using the new ceramics

Medical implants

Because body fluids do not dissolve the new ceramics, these superhard materials make ideal artificial bone and joint implants. Ceramic implants containing calcium fuse with surrounding bone.

Ceramic joints

Ceramics at home

Scissors and knives made of the tough new ceramics stay razor-sharp and never rust.

Refining old techniques to make superceramics

The ultrapure powders and precise firing techniques used to make the new ceramics produce a crystalline structure *(below, left)* finer and more regular than that of conventional ceramics *(below, right).*

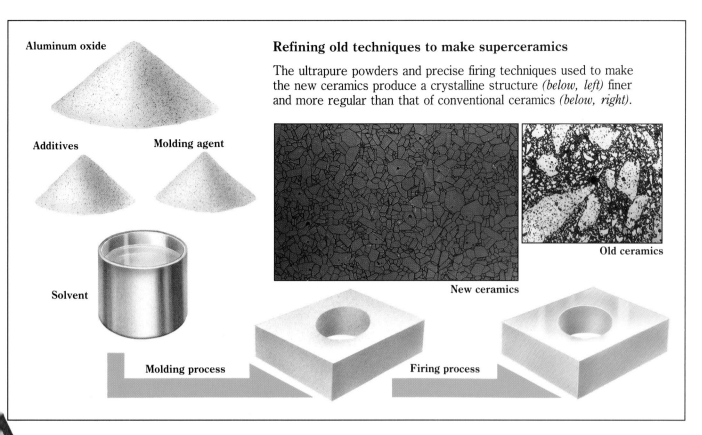

Aluminum oxide

Additives

Molding agent

Solvent

Molding process

Firing process

New ceramics

Old ceramics

Keeping the shuttle cool

The underside of the space shuttle's fuselage and wings *(left)* is armored with heat-resistant new ceramic tiles to prevent overheating. During reentry, friction between the shuttle and the air can generate temperatures of 1,245° C., or 2,300° F.

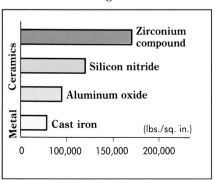

Space shuttle

Metal's new competitors

Certain advanced ceramic materials outperform cast iron, aluminum, and steel in tests of stiffness, or resistance to bending, and hardness, or the ability to withstand cuts; both are measured in pounds of pressure per square inch. They also resist heat well. These properties make ceramics the choice for many machine parts *(right).*

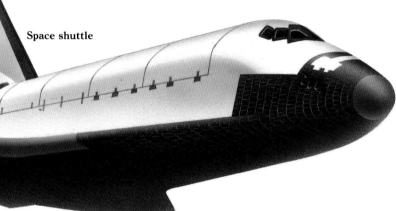

Resistance to bending

Ceramics

Metal

Zirconium compound

Silicon nitride

Aluminum oxide

Cast iron

(lbs./sq. in.)

0   100,000   150,000   200,000

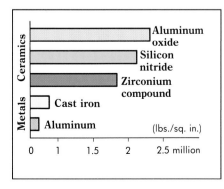

Hardness

Ceramics

Metals

Aluminum oxide

Silicon nitride

Zirconium compound

Cast iron

Aluminum

(lbs./sq. in.)

0   1   1.5   2   2.5 million

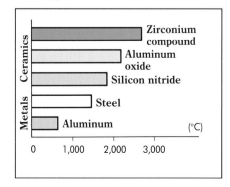

Melting point

Ceramics

Metals

Zirconium compound

Aluminum oxide

Silicon nitride

Steel

Aluminum

(°C)

0   1,000   2,000   3,000

How Are Synthetic Diamonds Made?

Diamonds—Earth's hardest natural substance—are prized for their brilliant sparkle. But they also are tough, corrosion-resistant, and have electrical resistance and heat-channeling properties. These characteristics make diamonds ideal for industrial use. In engines, nuclear reactors, and drilling rigs, in space, and in the ocean, diamonds work in punishing environments where less stable materials quickly deteriorate.

Natural diamonds were forged long ago from carbon deposits in the hot, high-pressure folds of Earth's mantle and are mined at great effort and expense. Demand for natural diamonds, not sur-prisingly, has always exceeded supply. But in the late 1950s, scientists simulated the temperatures and pressures of Earth's interior in the laboratory to make the first synthetic diamonds.

Diamond manufacturers today have two ways of applying the intense heat and pressure needed to convert the loose, two-dimensional molecular structure of graphite—a form of carbon—into diamond's dense, three-dimensional crystal structure. Dynamic synthesis harnesses the energy of an explosion for instant transformation. Static synthesis, with its sustained high pressure *(below, left)*, works more slowly.

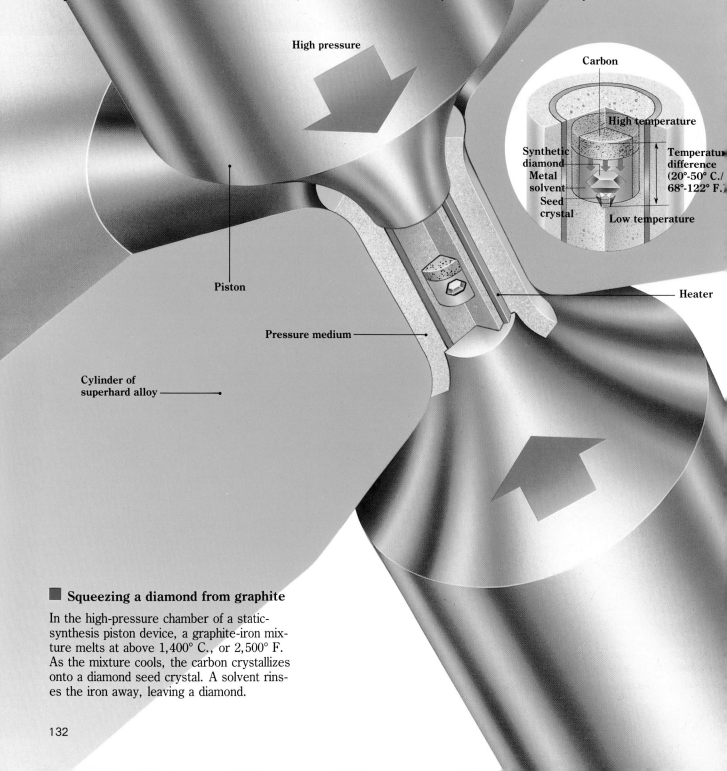

High pressure

Carbon

High temperature

Synthetic diamond

Temperature difference (20°-50° C./ 68°-122° F.)

Metal solvent

Seed crystal

Low temperature

Piston

Heater

Pressure medium

Cylinder of superhard alloy

▦ Squeezing a diamond from graphite

In the high-pressure chamber of a static-synthesis piston device, a graphite-iron mixture melts at above 1,400° C., or 2,500° F. As the mixture cools, the carbon crystallizes onto a diamond seed crystal. A solvent rinses the iron away, leaving a diamond.

A job for diamonds

Synthetic diamonds are used in offshore drilling rigs like this one to bore through miles of bedrock. Tiny as they are, synthetic diamonds *(far right)* with their cubic crystals have many cutting edges, and their hardness allows them to wear away otherwise impenetrable rock.

With its synthetic diamond teeth, this oil-drilling bit grinds through undersea bedrock.

The diamond line

A transition line *(red)* shows the conditions that produce synthetic diamonds. First graphite *(blue area)* is heated to above 1,400° C., or 2,500° F., at high pressure. Dropping the temperature slightly *(vertical line)* while maintaining the pressure nudges graphite over the transition line, turning it into diamond *(pink)*.

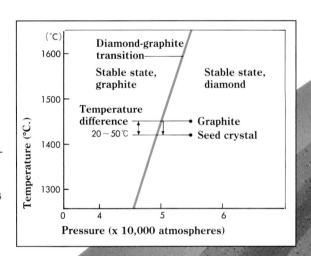

Earth as a diamond factory

Natural diamonds formed 100 million years ago in the mantle, a high-temperature, high-pressure region below Earth's crust. Volcanic eruptions flushed the diamonds from the surrounding rock, called kimberlite, into the upper crust.

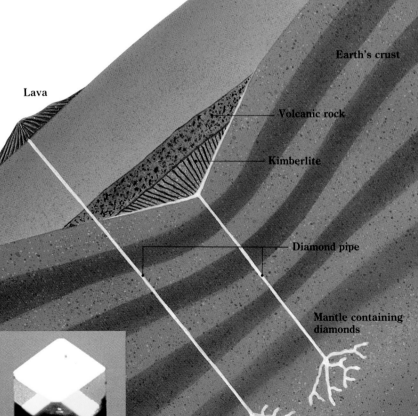

Lava

Earth's crust

Volcanic rock

Kimberlite

Diamond pipe

Mantle containing diamonds

▲ **Natural diamonds**

▲ **Synthetic diamond**

How Is Silicon Made for Microchips?

Today's electronics industry is built on the integrated circuit—a tiny chip of silicon engraved with as many as a million microscopic electronic switches for controlling electric current. Because silicon's crystalline structure can be made to carry a nearly infinite array of electric pathways, it has become a vital electronic resource.

Only the purest silicon, however, can serve these purposes. Natural silicon consists of differently oriented crystals grouped into polycrystalline grains. Where these grains meet, they form irregular boundaries that can disrupt electricity flowing across them. To get around this problem, scientists devised a way to produce single-crystal silicon, a substance with a crystalline structure so uniform that it will accept any electrical pattern imposed on it.

A recipe for purest silicon

Sand or silica rock

1 **The second** most plentiful element on Earth after oxygen, silicon occurs in silica rock *(above)* as silicon dioxide. Silica rock, including sand and quartz, makes up a quarter of Earth's crust.

Single-crystal silicon *(above)* is one solid crystal with no intercrystalline boundaries. Its atoms are uniformly bonded throughout.

Silicon crystal

Silicon atoms

4 **With the melted** silicon at 2,058° C., or 3,736° F., a seed of single-crystal silicon is lowered into the cauldron. Then as the seed is slowly rotated and withdrawn—in a way akin to dipping candles—silicon atoms in the liquid bind chemically to the turning seed in an orderly pattern *(above)*. The result is a crystal about 6 inches in diameter.

2 **To free** the silicon bound in silicon dioxide, the compound is heated with carbon to remove the oxygen. Elemental silicon remains.

Silicon

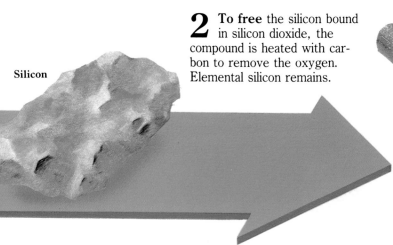

Polycrystalline silicon

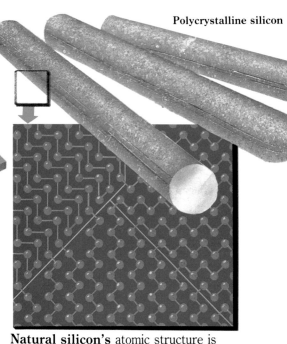

3 **Melting purified** silicon *(left)* allows its crystalline structure to be altered. Left to cool, it develops a compartmentalized, polycrystalline structure *(right)* that disrupts electric current.

Natural silicon's atomic structure is threaded by irregular crystal boundaries.

Single-crystal silicon

Melted high-purity silicon

The making of a chip

The single-crystal silicon cylinder is sliced into thin wafers, each .05 centimeter, or .02 inch, thick.

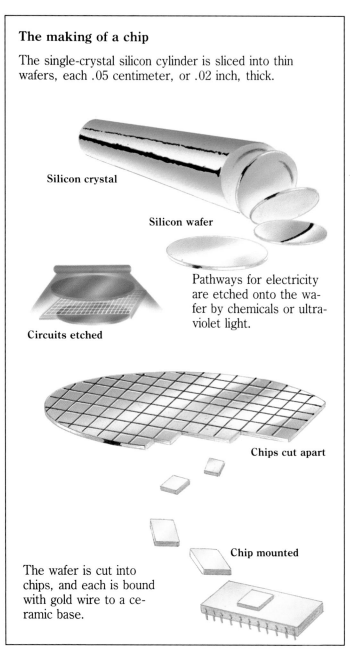

Silicon crystal

Silicon wafer

Pathways for electricity are etched onto the wafer by chemicals or ultraviolet light.

Circuits etched

Chips cut apart

Chip mounted

The wafer is cut into chips, and each is bound with gold wire to a ceramic base.

How Do Liquid Crystals Work?

Liquid crystals—the mysterious substances that form the numbers on a digital timepiece—pour like liquids but in other ways act like solids. The crystals are composed of rodlike molecules that, when stimulated by electric current, alter their orientation and either rotate light or let it pass through unchanged.

Inside any liquid-crystal display (LCD), such as a clock, are polarizing filters *(below)*, which block light. The filters are oriented at 90° angles. As light passes through the first polarizer, the crystals in their normal spiral pattern *(below, left)* rotate it 90°. The light then moves through the second polarizer, hits a mirror, and is sent back out as the bright background of the display. But when current is applied to liquid-crystal molecules *(below, right)*, they realign and do not rotate incoming light. Dark areas appear on the display, forming numerals according to different combinations of charged and uncharged areas.

Since an LCD reflects rather than generates light, it uses very little electricity.

Forming numbers out of darkness

Transparent digit segments *(below and right)* are etched into an electricity-conducting layer in the glass of the display. When current is applied to a segment *(far right)*, the crystals do not rotate and light is blocked.

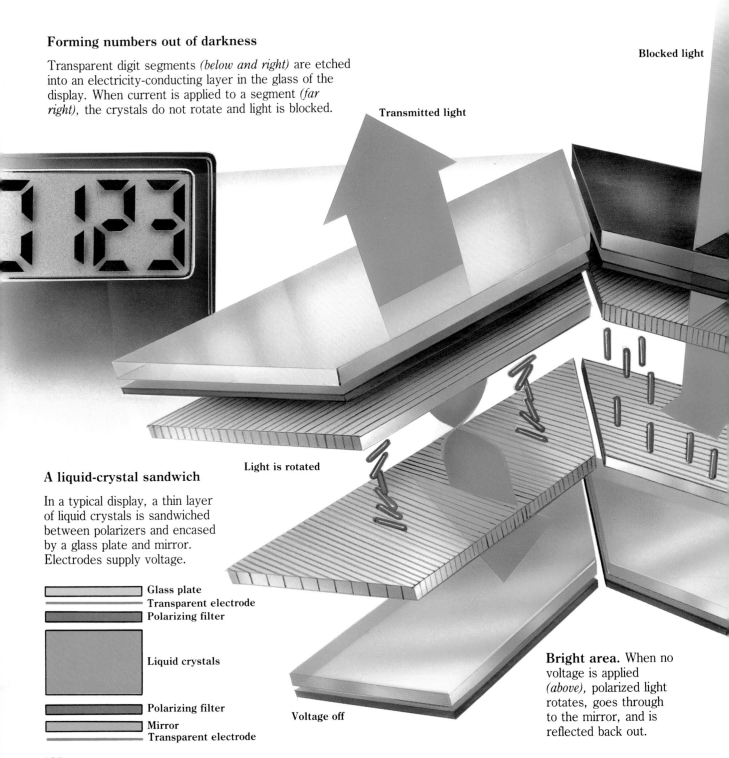

Blocked light

Transmitted light

Light is rotated

A liquid-crystal sandwich

In a typical display, a thin layer of liquid crystals is sandwiched between polarizers and encased by a glass plate and mirror. Electrodes supply voltage.

Glass plate
Transparent electrode
Polarizing filter

Liquid crystals

Polarizing filter
Mirror
Transparent electrode

Voltage off

Bright area. When no voltage is applied *(above)*, polarized light rotates, goes through to the mirror, and is reflected back out.

Molecular patterns

The three main types of liquid crystals are classified according to their molecular alignment *(right)*. Chemists exploit each pattern in designing uses for liquid crystals. LCDs use nematic or cholesteric liquid crystals.

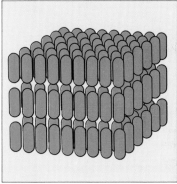

Smectic crystals stand on end, forming layered rows.

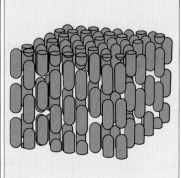

Nematic crystals cluster in staggered parallel lines.

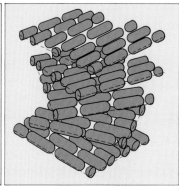

Cholesteric crystals form offset pivoting stacks.

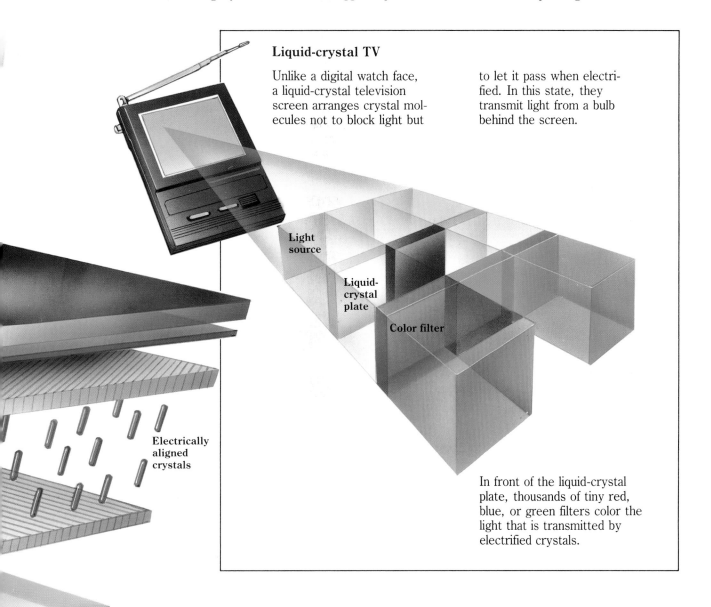

Liquid-crystal TV

Unlike a digital watch face, a liquid-crystal television screen arranges crystal molecules not to block light but to let it pass when electrified. In this state, they transmit light from a bulb behind the screen.

Light source

Liquid-crystal plate

Color filter

In front of the liquid-crystal plate, thousands of tiny red, blue, or green filters color the light that is transmitted by electrified crystals.

Electrically aligned crystals

Voltage on

Dark area. When voltage is applied *(above)*, the light travels straight along the reoriented crystals and is blocked by the second polarizer.

Hot and cold molecules

A liquid crystal's molecular arrangement changes in response not only to electric impulses but also to temperature variations. Using compounds that refract light of different colors *(right)* at different temperatures, chemists have devised thermometers for medical, industrial, and home uses.

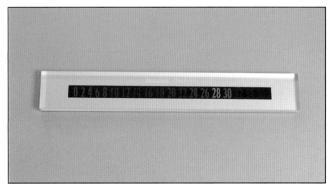

How Are Carbon Fibers Used?

Carbon fiber is thinner than ordinary cotton thread but three times as strong as steel. It is made by heating an organic polymer yarn, such as rayon, pitch, or other polymers—materials with very large, long, cross-linked molecules—in ovens at about 2,500° C., or 4,500° F. This drives out atoms of other substances such as hydrogen and oxygen and allows carbon atoms to link together into a more involved crystalline structure. The resulting fibers are at once extremely strong and exceptionally elastic.

By themselves, however, carbon fibers are hard to manipulate. To further strengthen the fibers and make them easier to mold, manufacturers bond them with an epoxy resin, a plastic glue that hardens as it cures. Injected into a hollow mold, the plasticized fibers are left to harden.

Most carbon fibers are used in plastic composites to make sporting goods such as tennis rackets, golf clubs, and fishing poles, as well as boat hulls, racing-car and aerospace components. Since these materials can be injection-molded into complex, precise shapes in one step, they are cheaper to use than metals. A composite part is also sturdier than metal, which must be bent, joined, and welded to form the same shape.

Versatile carbon fibers

Ultrafine carbon fibers are woven into tough, heat-resistant fabrics or bonded with epoxy resins to create strong structural elements to be used in jets, rockets, and high-performance racing cars, and also for a great variety of sporting goods.

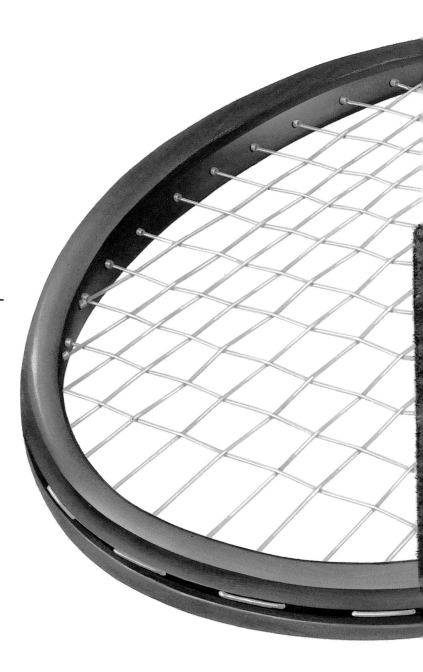

Stronger than steel and titanium and more flexible than metals or reinforced plastics, carbon fibers can stand up to a million pounds of pressure per square inch.

Chains of steely molecules

Some polymer fibers have a molecular structure that is netlike but has some loose ends *(left)*. Baking eliminates some elements, and the atoms rearrange into a net of strong hexagons *(bottom left)* with no loose ends.

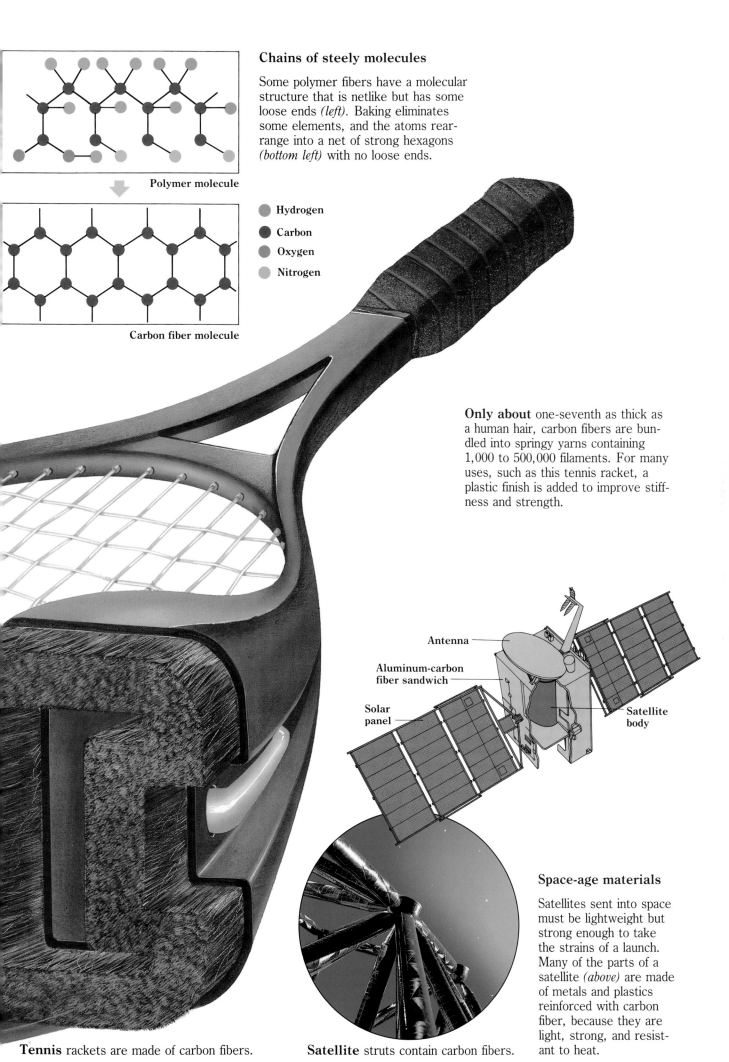

Polymer molecule

Carbon fiber molecule

- Hydrogen
- Carbon
- Oxygen
- Nitrogen

Only about one-seventh as thick as a human hair, carbon fibers are bundled into springy yarns containing 1,000 to 500,000 filaments. For many uses, such as this tennis racket, a plastic finish is added to improve stiffness and strength.

Antenna

Aluminum-carbon fiber sandwich

Solar panel

Satellite body

Space-age materials

Satellites sent into space must be lightweight but strong enough to take the strains of a launch. Many of the parts of a satellite *(above)* are made of metals and plastics reinforced with carbon fiber, because they are light, strong, and resistant to heat.

Tennis rackets are made of carbon fibers.

Satellite struts contain carbon fibers.

What Are Shape-Memory Alloys?

Once everyday metal wire has been twisted, it can only be straightened again with difficulty and will retain its kinks. A wire made of a shape-memory alloy, however, resumes its original form when heat is applied. The heat "reminds" it of its first crystalline structure.

All metals experience changes in bonding patterns at given temperatures and pressures. If a piece of simple metal is bent, for example, the crystalline lattice's atomic bonds slip, letting the lattice move; new links form, making the deformations permanent. But when a shape-memory alloy is bent or cooled below a given temperature, the angle of its atomic bonds shift without reordering the crystalline lattice. Though the alloy's overall shape may change dramatically, it regains its initial form—externally and molecularly—when heated.

Crystalline lattice when cooled

Shape-memory alloy phases

Cooling

Cooling. When cooled, the atoms of a shape-memory alloy alter their bonding angles but not their relative positions in the crystalline lattice *(above)*. Its outer shape does not change.

Lattice resumes original shape.

Heating

A repeatable cycle. A shape-memory alloy that is cooled or bent resumes its old shape when heated.

Heating. Heat restores the crystalline lattice of a deformed shape-memory alloy to its original form.

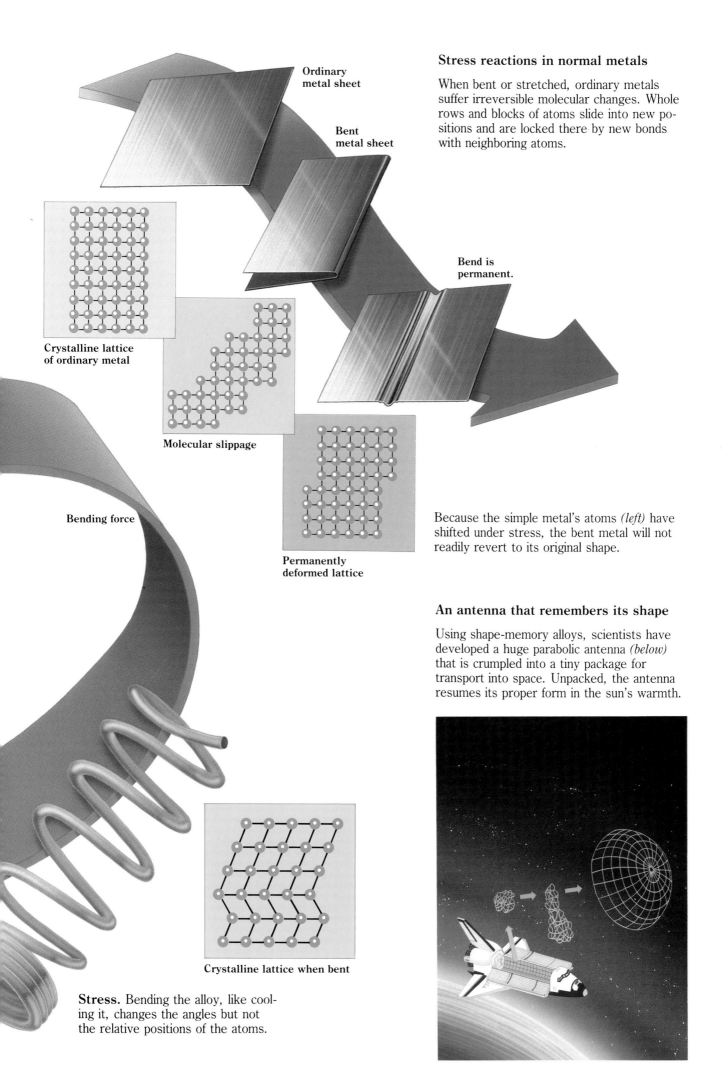

Stress reactions in normal metals

When bent or stretched, ordinary metals suffer irreversible molecular changes. Whole rows and blocks of atoms slide into new positions and are locked there by new bonds with neighboring atoms.

Ordinary metal sheet

Bent metal sheet

Bend is permanent.

Crystalline lattice of ordinary metal

Molecular slippage

Permanently deformed lattice

Because the simple metal's atoms *(left)* have shifted under stress, the bent metal will not readily revert to its original shape.

Bending force

An antenna that remembers its shape

Using shape-memory alloys, scientists have developed a huge parabolic antenna *(below)* that is crumpled into a tiny package for transport into space. Unpacked, the antenna resumes its proper form in the sun's warmth.

Crystalline lattice when bent

Stress. Bending the alloy, like cooling it, changes the angles but not the relative positions of the atoms.

Why Are Amorphous Metals Flexible?

The word *amorphous* means "without shape." An amorphous metal has none of the internal shapes—crystalline boundaries—seen in ordinary metals. Instead, its atomic arrangement is smooth and consistent throughout. Metallurgists developed amorphous metals in the 1960s by speeding up the cooling of a molten metal.

Molten metal is a fluid mix of randomly bonded atoms. When the melt cools slowly, crystalline structures grow all through the material as it solidifies, forming a tightly organized, repeating network of crystalline cells. Flash-cooling molten metal freezes the atoms in place before molecular forces can organize them into a crystal lattice. Free from grain boundaries and other gaps in molecular structure, amorphous metals are less prone to cracks, shearing, and magnetic or electric distortions. These properties make them ideal for use in magnetic recording heads and such electrical devices as transformers.

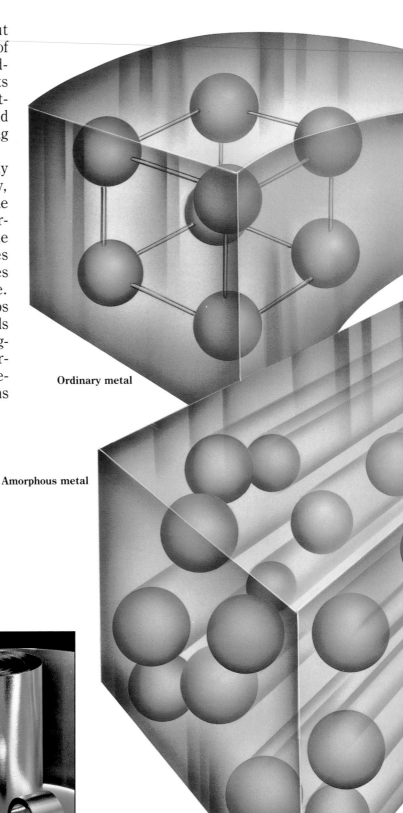

Ordinary metal

Amorphous metal

Lustrous ribbons of amorphous metal are flexible enough to be rolled up, because they can be made as thin as paper.

One substance, two products

The two metals below differ only in how fast they were cooled. Slow cooling produces normal metal *(top)* with its crystalline lattice; ultrafast cooling yields the less organized amorphous metal *(bottom)*.

Slow cooling

Rapid cooling

Molten metal

An inside look at amorphous and ordinary metals

A comparison of the arrangement of atoms of amorphous and ordinary metals *(below)* reveals striking differences. Amorphous metal's homogeneous, unbroken atomic arrangement accounts for its greater flexibility.

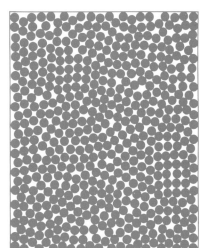

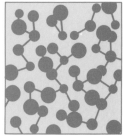

The microstructure of an amorphous metal *(below)* displays atoms arrayed in a seamless, random pattern *(left)*.

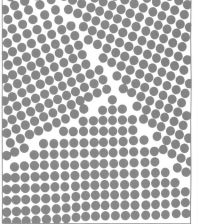

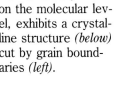

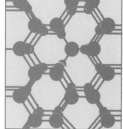

Normal metal, seen on the molecular level, exhibits a crystalline structure *(below)* cut by grain boundaries *(left)*.

Superchilled ribbons

To prevent crystal growth, molten metal must be cooled by a million degrees in one second. In one method, liquid metal is fed between superchilled rollers. The rollers flash-cool the melt, extruding paper-thin ribbons of amorphous metal.

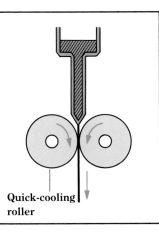

Quick-cooling roller

143

What Is Photosensitive Resin?

Some substances alter their chemical structure when exposed to light. One of these is photosensitive resin, a jellylike material made up of micromolecules resembling loose fragments of chain-link fence *(right)*. Under ultraviolet light, these molecules fuse into long, cross-linked macromolecules called polymers *(below)*. In bonding together, the polymers turn the gummy resin into a hard substance.

Such resins are used to make printing plates and microchip circuit patterns. In printing, a film negative is laid on a slab of photosensitive resin and flooded with ultraviolet light. The resin under the negative's transparent parts receives light and hardens, while the areas kept dark stay soft. The soft areas are rinsed away, leaving crisp forms duplicating the film images.

Creating patterns in resin

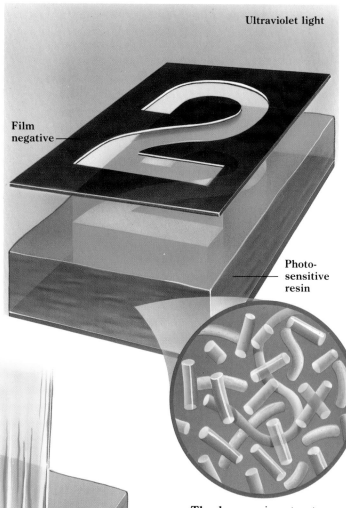

Ultraviolet light

Film negative

Photo-sensitive resin

The fused microstructure of resin exposed to light

The loose microstructure of resin shielded from light

Shapes cast by light

Wherever ultraviolet light hits a semisoft block of photosensitive resin *(top)*, the resin's molecules join into chainlike polymers *(left)*, hardening the gel.

Photosensitive resins are used to make difficult printing plates of detailed images.

Glossary

Acid: A corrosive substance that releases hydrogen ions when added to water. By definition, all acids measure less than seven on the pH scale.

Acid rain: Rain that contains strong concentrations of acid-forming chemicals such as sulfur dioxide.

Alkali: A compound that captures hydrogen ions from acids to form ionic salts. By definition, all alkalis register higher than seven on the pH scale.

Alloy: A compound of a metal, such as steel, mixed with either other metals or nonmetals.

Amino acid: An organic molecule with a distinctive chemical structure; some amino acids are the building blocks of proteins.

Amorphous metal: A type of metal with atoms that do not form the rigid crystals characteristic of conventional metals.

Anode: The negative electrode in an electric circuit where oxidation occurs.

Antimatter: Particles equal in mass but opposite in charge to given particles of matter. For example, the negatively charged antiproton is the antimatter counterpart of the proton, and the positron is the positively charged antiparticle of the electron.

Atom: The smallest piece of an element that still retains the chemical properties of that element. Atoms consist of two main parts: a central **nucleus** made of positively charged **protons** and neutrally charged **neutrons,** and an electron cloud made of negatively charged electrons orbiting around the nucleus.

Atomic number: The number of protons in an atom's nucleus.

Big Bang: The cataclysmic explosion some 4.6 billion years ago from which all space and matter sprang into being.

Blast furnace: A large, intensely hot oven used to smelt metal ores.

Bond: A connection between two atoms. The two main types of bonds are **ionic bonds,** in which electrons are transferred from one atom to another, creating oppositely charged ions, and **covalent bonds,** in which the atoms share electrons.

Buoyancy: An upward force equal to the weight of a substance, such as air or water, displaced by an object.

Carbon fiber: Filaments formed when a synthetic fiber, such as rayon, is seared in a very hot oven; the heat embeds grains of carbon into the fiber, making it very strong.

Catalyst: A substance that causes or increases the speed of a chemical reaction.

Cathode: The positive electrode in an electrical circuit where reduction occurs.

Ceramics: Substances containing clay and various minerals that become hard when fused by intense heat.

Chain reaction: In chemistry, a process in which particles released from one decaying radioactive nucleus induce other radioactive nuclei to decay, generating a cascade of decaying atoms.

Chemical reaction: Any process that involves a change in the composition of one or more substances.

Chemistry: The science dealing with the structure and composition of matter and the changes it undergoes.

Colloid: A mixture of two substances in which small particles of one substance are evenly dispersed throughout—but not dissolved in—another substance. The major types of colloids are **foams,** consisting of gas particles suspended in a solid; **emulsions,** consisting of liquid particles suspended in another liquid; and **aerosols,** consisting of solid particles suspended in a gas.

Compound: A substance composed of two or more elements bound together.

Compression molding: A method for making thermosetting resins in which the resin is added to a mold, then melted at high pressure to form the desired shape.

Concrete: A construction material that consists of three ingredients: **cement,** a mixture of chemicals such as alumina, silica, lime, iron oxide, and magnesia; **aggregate,** a mixture of sand and gravel; and water. When water is added, the cement forms a paste that sticks to the aggregate particles, forming a strong solid.

Converter: A device that lowers the carbon content of pig iron by exposing it to oxygen, which reacts with the iron's carbon to produce carbon monoxide.

Cryogen: Any substance that reduces the freezing point of the solvent in which it is dissolved.

Crystalline lattice: An orderly, repeating, three-dimensional pattern of atoms or molecules in a solid.

Direct reduction: The step in the refining of metal oxides in which carbon removes oxygen from the oxide, forming carbon monoxide and leaving behind pure metal.

Electrochemical cell: A mixture of chemicals that can provide an electric current when connected to a circuit; the current comes from electrons released when one chemical in the cell oxidizes and another reduces.

Electrolysis: The method by which an electric current is used to reduce the oxidized metal in ores.

Electrolytes: Compounds, usually ionically bonded, that fail to conduct electricity when solid but do so when liquid or in a solution.

Electromagnetism: A force of nature that encompasses the interactions of both electrically charged and magnetic substances.

Electroplating: The process in which an electric current is used to deposit a thin layer of pure metal onto an object.

Element: Any substance composed of a single type of atom. There are three types of elements: **metals,** such as gold and silver; **nonmetals,** such as oxygen and nitrogen; and **metalloids,** such as silicon and carbon.

Energy level: Any orbit in which the electrons surrounding an atomic nucleus may reside. The orbit of lowest energy level for a particular electron is called the **ground state.**

Epoxy resin: A polymer that acts as a strong adhesive when it is solid.

Equilibrium: The point in a chemical process at which there is no longer a net change in the amount of starting materials and products.

Fermentation: The reaction in which bacteria convert the sugars in food into either acids or alcohol.

Flavor enhancer: Any substance that increases the tongue's sensitivity to taste.

Fractional distillation: A procedure for separating a mixture of different liquids that exploits the fact that each liquid, called a **fraction,** has a different boiling point.

Glass: A transparent material made from silicon dioxide that has been melted and cooled in a way that prevents the molecules from forming an orderly, crystalline lattice.

Half-life: The time it takes for half of a radioactive substance to decay.

Heat of fusion: The heat required to turn a substance from a solid into a liquid.

Hydrocarbon: Any molecule that contains only hydrogen and carbon atoms.

Indirect reduction: The process in the refining of metal oxides in which carbon monoxide—formed through direct reduction—removes oxygen from the oxide.

Injection molding: A method for making thermoplastic resins in which the resin is melted, injected into a mold, and cooled.

Inorganic molecule: Any molecule that does not contain carbon.

Integrated circuit: A single silicon chip that contains a large number of electronic circuits.

Intermolecular forces: The cohesive force exerted among molecules of a compound; the strength of this force determines whether the compound will exist as a solid, liquid, or gas.

Ion: An atom or molecule that has either lost or gained electrons and is therefore electrically charged.

Ion exchange film: A membrane that allows only certain ions to pass through.

Isotope: Atoms of the same element that contain different numbers of neutrons in their nuclei.

Kinetic energy: A measure of an object's energy of motion; the faster an object moves, the greater its kinetic energy.

Micelles: Spherical structures formed by aggregations of molecules that are polar on one end and nonpolar on the other. When added to water, such molecules form micelles in which the nonpolar ends are contained inside the sphere with the polar ends exposed to the water.

Monomers: The individual molecules that can be combined in long chains to make polymers.

Neutrinos: Subatomic particles that have little or no mass and no charge and travel at the speed of light.

Nuclear fission: The process in which an atomic nucleus breaks up and releases energy.

Nuclear fusion: The process in which two atomic nuclei combine to form a larger atom, in the course of which a great deal of energy is released.

Nuclear reactor: A device that uses the heat released by nuclear fission to generate electricity.

Optical fiber: A glass filament through which signals are sent in the form of light beams. An optical fiber consists of two parts, both made of glass: an inner **core** and a surrounding outer layer called the **cladding.**

Ore: A compound in which a metal is bound chemically to other metals or nonmetals.

Organic molecule: Any molecule that contains carbon.

Oxidation: A process by which an atom loses electrons.

Periodic table: A chart that divides the known elements into groups according to their atomic structure and their chemical properties.

pH: A scale that quantifies the acidity or alkalinity of a substance; it ranges from 0—the most acidic—to 14—the most alkaline.

Phase change: The transition of a substance from one state—either solid, liquid, or gas—to another.

Photon: A unit of electromagnetic radiation; it has properties of both waves and particles.

Photosensitive resin: A type of soft plastic that becomes hard when exposed to ultraviolet light.

Pig iron: Iron that has a relatively high carbon content.

Plasma: A state of matter in which all the electrons of its atoms have been stripped away.

Plastic: A material made from special polymers, called **resins,** that have been melted and molded into a desired shape.

Polarity of a bond: A measure of how evenly two or more covalently bonded atoms in a molecule share their electrons. If the electrons are shared unevenly, the bond is said to be polar.

Polarity of a molecule: In polar molecules, some parts of the molecule will carry a partial positive charge, while other parts will carry a partial negative charge. When the charges are evenly distributed, the molecule is said to be nonpolar.

Polarizer: A filter through which only light waves with a particular orientation can pass.

Polymer: A large molecule consisting of a long chain of smaller molecules chemically joined end to end.

Protein: A polymer consisting of a chain of amino acids chemically joined end to end; proteins make up most of the tissues in the human body.

Pulp: A fibrous material made from wood chips that have been soaked in chemicals and water; it is the base for papermaking.

Radioactivity: The rearrangement of an atomic nucleus to increase its stability, releasing high energy particles, or photons, in the process.

Radiocarbon dating: A technique for determining the age of ancient matter by measuring the amount of the isotope carbon 14 it contains.

Redox reaction: A chemical reaction in which one of the reactants undergoes oxidation and another undergoes reduction; these reactions form the basis of electrochemical cells.

Reduction: A process in which an atom gains electrons.

Respiration: The process in which a cell takes in oxygen for energy and releases carbon dioxide.

Semipermeable membrane: A filter with pores so small that only molecule-size particles may pass through it.

Shape-memory alloys: An alloy that will deform under pressure but return to its original shape when heated and the pressure is removed.

Slag: The waste material formed in the refining of metal ores.

Smelting: The process in which a metal ore is heated with oxygen or another gas to isolate the pure metal.

Solvent extraction: A procedure in which a desired compound is removed from a substance by immersing the substance in a solvent; the solvent dissolves the desired compound and leaves the rest of the substance behind.

Starch: A polymer consisting of numerous chemically joined glucose molecules.

Steam distillation: A process in which a compound is vaporized by exposure to steam; the steam induces the compound to vaporize at a temperature lower than its boiling point.

Strong nuclear force: The force that binds together the protons and neutrons in an atom's nucleus.

Subatomic particles: Particles that combine to make up atoms. Some examples are quarks—which combine in threes to create protons and neutrons—and electrons and neutrinos. There are more than 50 kinds of subatomic particles.

Sublimation: The process by which a substance changes directly from a solid to a gas.

Synthetic fibers: Fibers made from polymers that have been drawn out into long threads and spun together.

Temperature: An indirect measurement of the average speed of vibration of the molecules of a substance.

Thermoplastic resins: Plastics that lose their shape when heated.

Thermosetting resins: Plastics that, once formed, will not change their shape under heat.

Ultraviolet radiation: A type of electromagnetic radiation with wavelengths shorter than those of visible light.

Wavelength: The distance between consecutive crests of a wave.

Index

Staff for
UNDERSTANDING SCIENCE & NATURE

Assistant Managing Editor: Patricia Daniels
Editorial Directors: Allan Fallow, Karin Kinney
Writer: Mark Galan
Assistant Editor/Research: Elizabeth Thompson
Editorial Assistant: Louisa Potter
Production Manager: Prudence G. Harris
Senior Copy Coordinator: Jill Lai Miller
Production: Celia Beattie
Library: Louise D. Forstall
Computer Composition: Deborah G. Tait (Manager), Monika D.
   Thayer, Janet Barnes Syring, Lillian Daniels

Special Contributors, Text: Joseph Alper, John Clausen, Barbara C.
   Mallen, Gina Maranto, Jennifer J. Veech, Mark Washburn
Research: Patricia N. Holland, Jennifer J. Veech
Design/Illustration: Antonio Alcalá, Caroline Brock,
   Nicholas Fasciano, Catherine D. Mason, Stephen Wagner,
   David Neal Wiseman
Photography: Title page: Zambelli Internationale Fireworks. 41: Bob
   Roberts/Superstock. 54-55: NASA LBJ
Index: Barbara L. Klein

Consultants:
   Dr. Theodore Perros is a professor of chemistry and forensic
   science at George Washington University in Washington, D.C.
   Andrew Pogan is a high-school teacher of chemistry and physics
   in Montgomery County, Maryland.

Library of Congress Cataloging-in-Publication Data
Structure of matter.
      p.   cm. — (Understanding science & nature)
   Includes index.
   Summary: Discusses the structure and nature of matter and
ways in which it can change.
   ISBN 0-8094-9662-3 (trade) — ISBN 0-8094-9663-1 (lib. bdg.)
   1. Chemistry—Juvenile literature.
   2. Materials—Juvenile literature.
   [1. Matter.   2. Chemistry.]
   I. Time-Life Books.   II. Series.
   QD35.S77   1992
   540—dc20   92-12082
                                                  CIP
                                                   AC

TIME-LIFE for CHILDREN ™

Publisher: Robert H. Smith
Associate Publisher and Managing Editor: Neil Kagan
Assistant Managing Editor: Patricia Daniels
Editorial Directors: Jean Burke Crawford, Allan Fallow,
   Karin Kinney, Sara Mark, Elizabeth Ward
Director of Marketing: Margaret Mooney
Product Managers: Cassandra Ford, Shelley L. Schimkus
Director of Finance: Lisa Peterson
Financial Analyst: Patricia Vanderslice
Administrative Assistant: Barbara A. Jones
Special Contributor: Jacqueline A. Ball

Original English translation by International Editorial Services Inc./
C. E. Berry

Authorized English language edition © 1992 Time Life Inc.
Original edition © 1990 Gakken Co. Ltd. All rights reserved.
No part of this book may be reproduced in any form or by any electronic or mechanical means, including information storage
and retrieval systems, without prior written permission from the
publisher, except that brief passages may be quoted for reviews.

First printing. Printed in U.S.A.
Published simultaneously in Canada.
Time Life Inc. is a wholly owned subsidiary of
THE TIME INC. BOOK COMPANY.
TIME-LIFE is a trademark of Time Warner Inc. U.S.A.
For subscription information, call 1-800-621-7026.